GETTING TO THE TOP

EMMANUEL ANNING

Getting to the Top
Copyright © 2023 by Emmanuel Anning

Published by
Sophos Books
163 Warbank Crescent
Croydon
CR0 0AZ

All rights reserved. No part of this publication may be reproduced, stored in a retrieval system, or transmitted in any form or by any means, mechanical, electronic, photocopying or otherwise without the prior written consent of the copyright owner.

ISBN 978-1-905669-79-0

Unless otherwise stated, all scriptures are taken from the King James Version of the Bible.

Cover design by Icon Media
Printed in the United Kingdom

CONTENTS

Dedication   5

Acknowledgements   7

Foreword   11

Why This Book?   15

1. Getting to the Top   19
2. What Is Isolation?   49
3. Why Isolation?   59
4. Information   77
5. Skill   89
6. Opportunity   103
7. Leadership   130
8. Attitude   157
9. Thriving   175
10. Influence   191
11. Order   209
12. Negotiation   243

*I dedicate this book to Amy, Kim and
Josiah, my biggest congregation.
God bless you guys!*

Acknowledgements

Writing this book was more of a challenge than I thought it would be. It was also rewarding beyond my imagination. None of this would have been possible without my best friend, Edward Addison. He was the first person I thought of when I started this project. His service to my family and his friends, and the impact of his ministry over our lives, shows true servanthood. It is unparalleled! I celebrate you greatly, sir.

I am eternally grateful to Richard Aryeetey. Your services to Archbishop Charles Agyinasare,

Founder of *Perez Chapel International* and the body of Christ are exemplary for the next generation of leaders. Thank you, and God bless you, my brother. To Godfrey Ocran, who served me so faithfully as my resident Pastor in *Fountain House Chapel International, Luton*, over many years. You worked hard behind the scenes to create a joyful and peaceful church, supporting Fountain House Chapel's vision with pure loyalty and commitment. Man of God, I am incredibly grateful.

A special thanks to my resident Pastor in *House Chapel Ghana*, Seth Bekoe, for his dedication, commitment, and hard work. For every sacrifice you have given, God has got you covered! You are God's general in the making. I acknowledge the dedication of many pastors I know serving in local churches worldwide. Your commitment is never in vain. I sincerely want to acknowledge Pastor Prince Kweku Dontoh (*Grace Garden Church, Accra*), Frank Ntim, Robert Kofi Gray, and Bright Boateng; you guys have done brilliantly behind closed doors. I gleaned a lot from you as I was writing this book. Remember, you are in isolation, and God is up to something.

To the First Lady of *Fountain House Chapel International, Rosemond*, God bless you for your effort and hard work behind the scenes of the ministry. May God reward you eternally and grant you the strength to carry on with the mandate you have received from the Lord.

Foreword

The path to the top is strewn with curveballs threatening to abort the vision God has placed in our hearts. However, the difficulties we encounter along the road to success are often tools in the hands of God to prepare us to walk in the corridors of power and accomplish all that He intends for us.

No one achieves anything of significance without the vital element of preparation. Although a crucial part of success, preparation can be a lonely road where your gifts and talents are not celebrated, and the challenges you face empower you for the task ahead.

For about four decades in ministry, I have observed many gifted and talented people short-circuit their destinies and fail to enter what God designed for them, or they achieve little because they were simply unprepared for the task. Indeed, there is no shortcut to greatness. We cannot achieve anything significant without hard work. Prayer has its place, and the grace of God is essential, but adequate preparation is vital. As the writer, Rev Dr Emmanuel Anning, succinctly puts it, 'There is a place, a time, and a season for preparation.' It is in isolation that God moulds and shapes you for greater works.

In this book, Getting to the Top, Dr Anning shows the reader that the place of isolation should not be considered as a punishment, but rather the place for gaining knowledge, developing skills, dying to self, emerging as an effective leader, and developing the right attitude needed for the top. The author has successfully gone through these stages of life and can write from personal experience.

This book carries a timely message for all who seek to attain the heights destined by God. It puts into perspective the challenges we encounter in the world and encourages the reader not to abandon the place of isolation, for it has great benefits. Greatness, innovation, and creativity are born in the womb of isolation. Change your attitude towards this lonely road and become the person God created you to be.

This book is a must-read for anyone who wants to live a life of purpose and reach the highest echelons of success in ministry, business, career, and education, to mention a few. Through this book, Dr Anning has placed the keys to developing influence and sustaining significance into your hands. I highly recommend it to you and your community of friends.

Shalom!

Bishop Jonathan Ekuban (PhD)
Senior Pastor
Springs of Life Chapel International
Accra, Ghana

Why This Book?

Moving to the Top is my first printed book after several publishers had rejected my manuscripts. The discouraging statements about the grammar and content made me feel inadequate. There were nights and days I couldn't sleep because I wondered why nobody believed in my gift. Why couldn't they see my unique gift? As I had flashes of inspiration, I simply wrote them down. I was eager to share what I believed were profound words of wisdom. Friends, publishers, and even those I sought to proofread my work ridiculed it. It was one of the most frustrating moments of my life.

I knew I had quality messages to dish out to the world. Yet, I was made to feel like an underdog and a loser. I felt like the second best, a second-class human. However, these temporary setbacks did not deter me. Instead, the experience galvanised my confidence, and triggered a determination in me to reach the top. The isolation period served as a springboard to break the shackle those naysayers had put around my mind, belief, and confidence.

My story will resonate with you if you are like an underdog, the unknown associate who is never given an opportunity. Perhaps you are the forgotten member of your organisation. Don't be perturbed. This book, which is the second part of *Moving to the Top*, is to remind you that the best is yet to come. It aims to activate your confidence, particularly if you think you have not accessed great opportunities in life. After reading the book, you will understand that life is full of unexpected changes, and the valley, where nobody knows who you are, is your perfect place to dig deep. What you do every day matters more than what you do occasionally. Do not fear the winds of adversity because a kite rises against the wind, not with it. Never be afraid of trying something new. Remember, amateurs built Noah's ark, but professionals built the Titanic. Which of them survived the Atlantic ocean? Never give up! Great people are resilient; they are tough and quick to recover. You learn more from failure than from success, so do not let it stop you. Failure builds character. And the most dangerous risk is not doing what you want because you believe you can buy yourself the freedom to do it later.

GETTING TO THE TOP

There is no shortcut to the place of your destiny

Life is filled with many twists and turns, but the patient traveller will eventually arrive at his divine destination. Everybody I know is working hard to get to the top. And to be honest, there is nothing wrong in reaching for greater heights in life. This chapter will explore what it means to get to the top and how to get there. No one becomes great without putting in the work. Some had to pay a hefty price to attain greatness. Any victory you do not pay a price for is a compromise. It is said that "you cannot push anyone up a ladder unless he is willing to climb." But while you desire to be at the top, there is a place, a time and a season for preparation.

To get to the top, you need lots of premeditated preparation. And though it takes time, it is worth it. The longer the preparation, the greater the success. Hence, the depth of your preparation period determines the magnitude of your success and impact.

Some people become successful only to realise they have not prepared enough for success. Every achievement and triumph in life is accompanied with challenges. And how you survive the challenges is determined by the time you spent to obtain your goals. God often allows trials to break us in order to make us stronger. Sometimes, He takes you through challenging situations to bring out the best in you. These times will make you fit for the tough times ahead. People who endure their seasons of travail often become the golden keys to healing, helping, and serving others. Getting to the top is an amazing journey for those who believe they are destined for greatness. It is sometimes lonely, but you are never alone because the hand of God is always on you.

As noted, on your journey to the top, you will

encounter diverse challenges, which are tailored to make you resilient and tough. In addition to being a learning period, the challenges will strengthen your faith in God. It is a season where you must learn to rest on God's sufficiency until He grants you breakthrough. The difference between great people and successful people is preparation. And prayerful preparation prevents poor performance.

Oftentimes, preparation happens because you have been shut in a place of isolation. Many great and talented leaders are on the 'island of the unknown', desperate to be known, seen, and heard. But that phase is to model, develop and brand them ahead of the future. Before the advent of modern technology, photography was developed in a darkroom. Similarly, in our days, God prepares His generals in a place of isolation. What you are currently experiencing is for a purpose. And since no great technology is created unexpectedly, don't be too quick to discard your dream. Those dreams will soon manifest into a glorious reality.

The Island of the Unknown

A winning lifestyle begins with preparation. And the preparations are often done in a place I call 'the island of the unknown'. As an avid fan of sports, I wonder why athletes train behind closed doors. From boxing to football and other sports, all the great sports people set camps outside their comfort zones and homes to train. They isolate themselves so they can prepare for victory. You may be in isolation right now, but your day of reckoning beckons. Preparation gives room for greatness. And even though the time and effort you put in are not convenient, the result is amazing. Whether you are a preacher, a manager, a doctor or a sportsperson, you will be isolated at some point. You might not know it at the moment, but it is a place of destiny.

Apostle Paul wrote a large part of the New Testament while he was in prison. The book of Revelation was written on the Island of Patmos. Your darkest hour, when you think God has deserted you, could be the perfect moment for preparation. God will take you out of the crowd to get the best out of you. Many of the famous people we admire today were once unknown. They were in a state of oblivion and isolation until they were brought to the limelight. Whenever you find yourself in the island of the unknown, remember that you are on your way to greatness. John was exiled to the island of Patmos near the end of Emperor Domitian's reign. Nevertheless, he wrote the book of Revelation, the last book in the Bible, at Patmos. John's story confirms that you can receive revelation in isolation and refinement in confinement. It is a place where your story becomes your glory and your limitations become manifestations.

You should not regret your period of isolation. It is a precious season for anyone aiming for the top. Consider Moses in the Old Testament, who was destined to be one of the greatest leaders of all time. God had to prepare him at the backside of the wilderness.

> *Now Moses kept the flock of Jethro, his father-in-law, the priest of Midian: and he led the flock to the backside of the desert, and came to the mountain of God, even to Horeb.* **Exodus 3:1**

Moses might have been despondent about the preparation period, but the results were incredible. He was prepared to lead God's children, the Israelites. Your preparation period may not correlate with your expectations, but it is enough to create the future you are destined for. Having endured the preparation phase, Moses wrote the first five books of the Bible. He led over two million slaves out of Egypt, one of the developed nations of old. God groomed him to set the template for parliament and the structures for law and governors. He was a great political leader in his generation. Moses cannot be compared with politicians who studied political science at the university. Because beyond the education of men, God confined and refined him for a purpose.

You may be in a state of absolute oblivion at the moment; don't be in a hurry. You will soon rise to stardom. The pain and preparation of today will determine tomorrow's echoes of greatness. There is no lasting glory won without a struggle. And you won't arrive at your destination in life on a platter of gold. You must get ready for the journey. When you are in an unfamiliar territory and you feel isolated, let your motto be, "My best is yet to come." No man arrives at the top by mistake because success is deliberate, victory is premeditated, and triumph is calculated.

As you embark on the journey to fulfilling your dreams, visions and aspirations, you will get to an unfamiliar and uncomfortable land, where you must toughen up against the vicissitudes of life. Why did God keep Moses at the backside of the wilderness? How was Moses supposed to save the enslaved children of Israel from Egypt, a powerful nation without military training? In place of military preparation, God isolated him in 'the island of the unknown'. He was kept in a place where the world seemed to have l forgotten him. It might seem like God has forsaken you too, but He is only preparing you for great and mighty things to come. As rightly said by Robert H. Schuller, "A spectacular achievement is always preceded by unspectacular preparation."

Some people want to achieve great things in life yet they refuse to serve or understudy others. Moses grew up in Pharaoh's palace, but he was made in the house of Jethro, a shepherd. Life may have begun well for you, but you may be groomed in the most unlikely places. You must understand that God doesn't do accidents, incidents, or misfortunes. He makes all things beautiful in His time. Even when you are in a place of isolation like Moses was, God's got you covered. As written in Deuteronomy 31:6 (NIV), "Be strong and courageous. Do not be afraid or terrified because of them, for the Lord your God goes with you; he will never leave you nor forsake you."

From the Back Seat to the Front Seat

After my pastoral training, when I went back to my local church, I was made to sit at the back of the church for several months. It was quite humiliating at the time because it seemed my local church did not accept or recognise me as a pastor. Regardless, I never missed a Sunday or weekday service. On a particular Sunday morning, while I sat at the back as usual, enjoying the service, I realised the head pastor needed someone to introduce him to the pulpit before he preached. Oftentimes, when there's no pastor or minister to be the master of ceremony who would usher in a preacher, the preacher would just head straight to the pulpit. But surprisingly, my pastor walked all the way to where I was seated and asked me if I could handle the master of ceremony role for the service.

The experience humbled me and taught me an invaluable lesson about moments of truth in life. I had spent many years waiting for that opportunity to come. And when I least expected, my moment of truth happened. But before it did, I was in a place of preparation. I was a shy person by nature; nobody believed I could preach. I attended a poor school by all standards and never looked like a 'superman' of God in the making. I never prophesied or saw visions like my peers. I was not even the most handsome or the most intelligent lad around. And I didn't look like quality material in the ministry.

But during my years in isolation, I practised preaching, public speaking, and how to handle oneself before a crowd. Even though I had no real audience then, I improvised. I used to pray in the woods back then. I would preach to the trees and anything in sight as though they were the congregation or audience. I would also lead them to Christ, minister to the sick, and make altar calls. I practised how to be a master of ceremonies and how to anchor opening and closing prayers. Nobody knew what I was doing; I never discussed it with anybody. But I now understand that though one's preparation at the backside of the desert might be unpleasant, it is the manual to reach the top.

At the Bible college I attended, I was above my peers. It was not because I was the most gifted, anointed or powerful, but I had been drilled and schooled in an isolated place. I rose to the top at the college and eventually became the student body's president. When preparation meets a destined opportunity, the result is exaltation. So, when I was at the backside of the church, I was waiting for my predestined time. What if, when the time came, I had no training on how to handle a massive audience? What if, when my pastor called, I fumbled with words or became nervous at the size of the congregation? I bless God that neither of these happened because I had laid the groundwork for the future.

Many are waiting for their big time, but they shy away from the big-time preparations. As I sat at the back of the church for months, I knew my time would come. My question to you is who do you want to become? A great pastor, manager or business owner? Do you want to be an amazing wife, husband or author? What efforts have you made towards your dreams? When my pastor walked to the back of the church and leaned over to make that request, I didn't think it was a big deal. But those five minutes I stood before the congregation that Sunday morning turned my life around. As I stepped down from the podium to return to my seat, the pastor said, "Emmanuel, you do not need to sit at the back anymore. From today, you will sit with the pastors in front of the church."

Perhaps, like me, you are sitting at the back in your workplace, church or school. It might look like an irrelevant place to be, but your season of opportunities will soon come. Ensure you do not fall short of your destined moment. As I noted, my life changed from that day. In the same place I was not recognised, my story was altered for good. If given the same opportunity, some people might do better than I did, but the point is I spent countless times in the woods practising for that moment (which may or may never come). But regardless of the uncertainty, I was determined to improve myself and prepare for the future anyway. Even if the day at the church never came, the experience I had gotten from constant practice would have been helpful in other situations — birthday party of a friend or short speech at work. At different intervals, life will bring many opportunities your way; be vigilant and sensitive because a lost opportunity can never be regained.

The Story Changed

I never wanted to be popular, but I always looked forward to being a blessing to my generation. Before I wrote my first book, when I was in school, I used to write short articles and post them on the notice board. The articles had lots of grammatical errors. I didn't belong to any writer's club or writing group nor did I have any formal training in writing. But I had a strong desire to write articles and short sermons. By the end of the day, the handwritten article would have lots of corrections from my readers and critics. I would take it, correct the errors, and repost it the following day. I was teased and mocked; many people laughed at my effort. However, I never gave up. One of my friends used to visit me in my single-room apartment, and he would see pieces of paper all over the place. He also made fun of me, and even though I was losing it as almost everyone did not believe in my dreams, I kept honing my skills.

But today, I can proudly say the story has changed. The guy who was once taunted for writing imperfect articles is now an author. Perseverance is such an awesome attribute in life. My story proves the aphorism that if you only knock long enough and loud enough at the gate, you are sure to wake up somebody. Don't allow your flaws to dim your shine. Regardless of what the world says, your dream is valid.

The first time I met a publisher was back at home in Africa. When he looked at my manuscript, he said there was no substance in the book, and it didn't make sense to him. The words felt like ice on my face. One of my principles in life is to try and fail, but don't fail to try. Rejections and failure might come your way, but no one will accuse you of not trying at all. I have no doubt that everyone is destined to succeed. But anyone who wants to make it in life must never despise the days of small beginnings. In spite of the bouts of discouragement on my path, my eyes were fixed on the good side.

You may find yourself at the deep end of the world, but your story will change if you don't give up. Although David was destined to be a king, he never grew up in the palace. He was living at the backside of the desert. He was neither in a royal camp outside the city nor in some palace being trained to become the next king. As a shepherd boy, he was alienated from comfort and overlooked by many. Even Samuel never thought he could be the king when God sent him to David's family.

> *"When they arrived, Samuel saw Eliab and thought, "Surely the Lord's anointed stands here before the Lord." But the Lord said to Samuel, "Do not consider his appearance or his height, for I have rejected him. The Lord does not look at the things people look at. People look at the outward appearance, but the Lord looks at the heart."* **1 Samuel 16:6-7**

Instead of being bitter or cynical about the fact that he had to tend his father's sheep while his elder brothers followed Saul to war, he grew bolder and stronger in what seemed like an isolated place. This means isolation can boost your determination to succeed in life. If you observe well, you will discover that when someone is left alone to survive in a lonely place, the person will develop some strength and determination to survive. Right in the wilderness, David killed a lion and a bear that carried off a sheep from his father's flock. God used that experience to train him ahead of the big fight with Goliath.

God has a way of setting up his people to be trained, educated and cultivated in the loneliest and deserted realm. To humans, it is ludicrous that instead of choosing one of David's brothers, who were of great stature, experienced in leadership and combat, God preferred a lad, who could not handle a sword, as a king. But in reality, David had been groomed into a general and great commanding officer by his experiences at the backside of the desert. When David was in isolation, nobody considered him. His father never bothered to invite him to partake in the sacrifice. He was forgotten by the very people who were supposed to love him and care about him. Yet when the day of appraisal arrived, they could not exclude him.

A time will come when even your opponents cannot discount you. They might have ridiculed you before, but when the work at the backside of the wilderness is accomplished, you will be amazed how things will realign to accommodate you.

There is a gentleman in our church in the United Kingdom who has been with us for some years. All along, I knew God had called him. He never raised his voice and never lobbied for any position in the church. He just did his job and served year after year. The first time I wanted him to preach in church, he strongly declined because he wasn't ready. I even tried to let him compère the service several times, but he refused. I'd always had a feeling that he was a great pastor in the making.

One day, I had to travel for a couple of weeks and, for some reasons, I felt it was his time. The week before I travelled, I made him preach on a weekday service. Everybody was amazed by the wisdom, grace, anointing and maturity that he demonstrated behind the pulpit. Isolation has a way of creating something out of nothing. Perhaps he never imagined himself getting close to the pulpit, but today he is our resident pastor, and a great one indeed. Don't ever underestimate yourself, especially what God can do through you afterwards, when you are in isolation. I have watched people become great leaders and captain-marvellous from nowhere. If you make yourself available, God will bring the best out of you.

According to 1 Samuel 16:11 (ESV) *"Then Samuel said to Jesse, "Are all your sons here?" And he said, "There remains yet the youngest, but behold, he is keeping the sheep." And Samuel said to Jesse, "Send and get him, for we will not sit down till he comes here."*

Keeping, in the emboldened words above, is synonymous with maintenance, custody, trust, charge and safekeeping. In isolation, there is always something you need to protect, maintain, guard and respect. Be careful so you don't underrate or take lightly what you have been entrusted with. We tend to underestimate the value of what we have until we lose it. David was responsible for taking care of sheep, and because he was not a soldier like his brothers, he was belittled. But that boy who was brushed aside turned out to be a great warrior and worshipper. Not only that but he was also a man after God's own heart (Acts 13:22, KJV).

People say talent is cheaper than table salt because not all talented individuals attain success. What separates a merely talented person from the successful one is a lot of hard work behind the scenes. You can argue that some talented people have a great family, but nothing can replace dedication.

Today, we have a "microwave" and "fast-food" generation. We just click a button, and all things are in sync. Nobody takes time to learn, read or even study anymore. We are heading towards a new generation of graduates who are less talented, not determined and can't persevere. At the backside of the wilderness, David — though unknown to him — was training for the moment with Goliath. Like him, you will eventually have the golden opportunity to face your Goliath. But if you have not prepared in the wilderness, how will you fight and conquer the enemy on the battlefield?

Isolation Precedes Launch into the Limelight

The Lord is wonderfully good to those who wait for him and seek him.
Lamentations 3:25

Although the word "isolation" is often associated with an unpleasant situation, I realise that God prepares his generals in such a place. There are six men in the Bible who were thrown into oblivion, but they later rose to the limelight. The men — Jacob, Moses, Jeremiah, Daniel, Paul and Jesus — were all alone at some point. But through their stories and many others after them, God has shown that obscurity can be a launch pad for popularity. To be alone is to be unaided, lonely, deserted, and isolated.

While I was writing this book, the Holy Spirit ministered a revelation about the acronym of the word "A.L.O.N.E" to me. Without a doubt, it is not easy to be left alone in an unfamiliar or isolated position, where you feel incarcerated or at a dead end. But then, you are never alone because that is the period where God wants you to develop yourself ahead of your journey. Although you might think God is silent at that moment, He is right there with you. If you pay attention, you will hear his whispers of encouragement.

A: Anointing

Whenever God isolates people for his purpose, He gives them an anointing, which constitutes the power of God and the manifestation of His presence. You and I are custodians of some kind of anointing that works in us depending on our assignment.

L: Led by the Spirit

Anyone thrown into isolation experiences the leading of the Holy Spirit. Being led by the Spirit is one of the most challenging journeys of the children of God because it requires a lot of sacrifices. You will fast, pray, wait and worship to hear the voice of the Spirit. You must also follow His leading as your divine guide and teacher; otherwise, you will fail if you rely on your strength. Being alone with God will fine-tune too, too.

O: Open

The experiences of great men and women open them up for success. Being isolated will open you up to numerous experiences. To fill a bottle with water, you must first remove the lid to allow access to the inside. Before God uses anyone, He will first put them in an isolated place to unlock and release their potential and gifts. Never underestimate this season because it opens you up to your God-given abilities.

N: New identity

When you find yourself alone in the pursuit of

your God-given assignment, a new "you" is created. After spending an alone time at the backside of the wilderness, Moses emerged a new person. When David was left alone to tend his father's sheep, the experience made him a new man. When Jacob was also left alone, an angel visited him, and He became a prince. He was a charlatan, but his alone time with God changed his name and story. Your seasons of loneliness are meant to make you a new person. To be alone is to welcome your "new identity".

E: Expression

As I was writing this book, my five-year-old son asked for the meaning of the word "expression". He might have heard it on a television advert. I tried to explain to him, but it was a little harder than I thought. I told him it is a look on somebody's face conveying a thought or feeling. So, he stood right in front of me and made some funny faces. Then he said, "Daddy, I am doing an expression". That funny but wholesome interaction made me understand that God teaches us the act of manifestation, demonstration and exhibition when we are in isolation. The athletes we watch and admire on the television are just expressing themselves through the sporting activities they engage in. But before then, they would have plunged into isolation to learn the act, rehearse and repeat it until they attain perfection. Your period of being alone is a dress rehearsal of the great day to come. Never underestimate your time in church as an associate pastor, usher, apprentice or as a servant in your workplace. It foreshadows the future. Greatness and potential are often nursed in isolation. It can also be likened to the incubation period; it is the time you invest in your growth.

Some of the men in the Bible who were left alone for some period

> *And Jacob was left alone; and there wrestled a man with him until the breaking of the day.* **Genesis 32:24**

1. Jacob

When life forces you into a place of isolation, never see it as a means to strip you of your dignity or self-esteem. Rather, it is a place of apprenticeship, where you grow and develop yourself. God has blessed this generation with an unprecedented increase in technological advancements and development. But nothing can replace the potency of apprenticeship. No successful person attains success all by themselves. Success is the outcome of accumulated preparation and trials. They would undergo the period of incubation, gestation and development before they become successful. People may not know your credentials today, but you are in an incubator and soon, you will shine forth. When Jacob was left alone, he had an encounter that transformed his life. The previous con man became the central figure of the Bible.

Genesis 32:27-28 read thus: "*And he said unto him, what is thy name? And he said, Jacob. And he said, Thy name shall be called no more Jacob, but Israel: for as a prince hast thou power with God and with men, and hast prevailed.*" When a man is alone, he can see further into the future than a man on a mountaintop. Isolation is an incubator where greatness and creativity are born. When everybody left Jacob, he attracted the unbeatable presence of God, and he experienced a long-lasting change that made him the Prince of God. Before I wrote my first book, there were times I felt discouraged. But anytime I go to my closet, God would tell me that the great books and wisdom He has invested in me would be unleashed. Dear friend, your present location is not the end of the journey; your best is yet to come. Have you observed that invigilators are always silent when a test is ongoing? You are in an examination class right now; concentrate and get the job done. And in the end, God will turn your situation around for good.

2. Moses

And Moses alone shall come near the LORD: but they shall not come nigh; neither shall the people go up with him.
Exodus 24:2

There is a place in life where no one but you must access. The world often surrounds you when everything is good, but at some point, you will have to endure some trials alone. Many leaders ended badly because they had too many voices speaking to them; they never had time to think for themselves and sift through the numerous counsels. Sometimes, you have to be alone to attract the presence of God. When it came to the anointing and the official mandate, Moses was left alone! You don't need too many people when you are answering God's calling for your life. It is not every ministry, pastor, manager or organisation that will believe you. At times, you will be alone. Friends will desert you; family will let you down, and your spouse may even give up on you. But these happenings do not diminish the value of your assignment in life.

3. Jeremiah

I sat not in the assembly of the mockers, nor rejoiced; I sat alone because of thy hand: for thou hast filled me with indignation. **Jeremiah 15:17**

Jeremiah said he was mocked among the assembly of the mockers; he sat alone because "the hand of God" saturated him with indignation (righteous anger, strength, intensity and power). And the Lord said to him in verses 20 and 21: *"I will make you a wall to these people, a fortified wall of bronze; they will fight against you but will not overcome you, for I am with you to rescue and save you, declares the Lord. I will save you from the hands of the wicked and deliver you from the grasp of the cruel."*

Do not allow your challenges to define you. If

you can be defined, you can be confined. Challenges have hidden powers to help you, but they fail to help when you allow them to define you. Don't let isolation, rejection and negative responses affect the pursuit of your dreams. The first day I stood before people to speak, I was mocked. The first prayer meeting I led was a disaster. The first book I wrote was ridiculed; it had too many grammatical errors, and I was not comfortable giving it to a proofreader. Yet I didn't allow any of these to dampen my spirit. I spent days alone honing my skills. Years later, I have preached in the same places they once mocked me, and they gave me a standing ovation. What changed? I saw my isolation period as a processing factory. Now that the world has not discovered you yet, be filled with righteous anger, strength, intensity and power to learn and serve. Work on that gift, dream and vision until the appointed time.

4. Daniel

And I, Daniel, alone saw the vision: for the men that were with me saw not the vision, but a great quaking fell upon them so that they fled to hide themselves.

Therefore, I was left alone, and saw this great vision, and there remained no strength in me: for my comeliness was turned in me into corruption, and I retained no strength. **Daniel 10:7-8**

Certain factors will drive you on in life when everyone else has given up on you. These factors are the visions, the mandates and the dreams that were handed to you alone. In my ministry, people have deserted me when I needed them the most. I have met people who were only with me for what they were getting. But what has never left is the experience I had with God, the vision He dropped in my spirit, and the assignment he called me for. When all men desert you, go back to the vision from the times you were alone with God.

5. Paul

Throughout the New Testament, Apostle Paul recounted his experiences when he was left alone. In the court, information is not admissible unless you are an eyewitness. Many of us are going about with unfounded revelations, unconfirmed reports and unauthenticated tales. The validity of our purpose is not in our mega buildings, the cars we drive, our credentials, the clothes we wear or the kind of friends we associate with; rather, it is in the type of eyewitness we are.

This book is to challenge you to remain resolute in your isolation. For that which you have seen and heard cannot be taken from you. According to 1 John:1-4, *"That which was from the beginning, which we have heard, which we have seen with our eyes, which we have looked upon, and our hands have handled, of the Word of life. (For the life was manifested, and we have seen it, and bear witness, and shew unto you that eternal life, which was with the Father, and was manifested unto us;). That which we have seen and heard declare we unto you, that ye also may have fellowship with us: and truly our fellowship is with the Father, and with his Son Jesus Christ. And these things write we unto you, that your joy may be full."*

6. Jesus

Spending time alone with God rids our minds of distraction and enables us to focus on Him and hear His word. By abiding in Him, we enjoy intimacy with Him. Jesus spent time alone with God whenever he needed to refresh his inner man. Many times, he had to send the multitudes away in order to be alone with God. Luke 9:18 says, *"And it came to pass, as he was alone praying, his disciples were with him: and he asked them, saying, Whom say the people that I am?"*

This book is about moving to the top, but on your journey, you will be alone, isolated. Never give in to despair during these seasons. They are the perfect timing of grace and mercy.

7. John on the Island of Patmos

Patmos is a sterile island about 30 miles in circumference. It also means "my killing". The apostle who wrote the book of revelation was left alone to die. As a sterile island, Patmos was unfruitful. And being unfruitful means the following:

1. Unable to produce offspring; infertile.
2. Free from any living thing (plants, trees or even animals).
3. Plants and trees could not produce or bear seeds, fruit, spores, stamens, or pistils.
4. It is a place of lack of inspiration, creativity, vitality and fruitfulness.

5. A place of no pasture, rocky, barren and desolate system.

How interesting that God would use such a place to reveal Jesus Christ to John! The Bible also revealed that David wrote the majority of his psalms at the time he was in isolation. Major revelations, inventions, innovations, and revolutions were borne in isolation. When we are alone, we must be discerning lest we miss a major revelation God wants to download in our heart. In this world of chaos and attention-driven activities, when you are on the island of Patmos, a deluge of life-changing revelations is about to be unleashed through you.

WHAT IS ISOLATION?

The tragedy in life doesn't lie in not reaching your goal. The tragedy lies in having no goal to reach.
- Benjamin Mays

Rough roads often lead to great heights. The final proof of greatness lies in one's ability to endure hardship and adversity without resentment. The evidence of your desire to move to the top is in your quest to read this book. The size of a man is determined by what he lives for and the price he is willing to pay to achieve that dream. In life, spectacular achievements are always preceded by unspectacular preparations. The desire to win is important, but the will to prepare is vital.

Abraham Lincoln said, "I will study and

prepare, and someday my chance will come". No greatness is born by accident! Many of the world's greatest personalities were furnished in a place called isolation. The dictionary defines "isolation" as:

1. The process of separating somebody or something from others, or the fact of being alone and separated from others.
2. Remoteness from other inhabited areas or buildings.
3. Separation, segregation, remoteness, loneliness and seclusion.
4. A lack of contact between persons, groups, or whole societies.

These definitions may not relate to your concept of greatness, but every spectacular achievement will require some amount of unglamorous means. The leaders of tomorrow are being furnished in the furnace of affliction at the backsides of life. When they emerge, we will adore and applaud them. The process that made them great is unceremonious, but the results are celebrated. You will have to spend time in absolute oblivion to prepare for your destiny. In

What Is Isolation? 51

isolation, you are lonely and sometimes forlorn, but greatness comes out of the season. This book is no formula book of success but a manual to help you in the land of isolation and to show you it is a period where preparation meets opportunity.

While the mediocre teacher tells, the good teacher explains. The superior teacher demonstrates, but the great teacher inspires. Isolation is a superior teacher. It is the battlefield where heroes are made. This book is not advocating a lifestyle of isolation or seclusion, but if you find yourself in such a place, it doesn't mean God has abandoned you. And it is a classroom of greatness.

Many subordinates know they have something to offer to their generation yet they are not recognised. But the key is patience because they are in an incubator, hence their mandate is in a caring and defensive stage. We get the chicken by hatching the egg, not by smashing it. Do you want to be at the top? Do you want to be celebrated? Do you want to arrive on the platform of greatness? Do you want to do great in life? If your answer is yes to these questions, life will first send you to a place of isolation. Are you prepared? Are you ready to ensure that phase where you are unknown and not celebrated?

If we have ever made any valuable discoveries or breakthroughs, it would have been a result of patience rather than just talent. Our blessings often appear to us in the shape of pains, losses, and disappointments in a place of isolation but when we are patient, we will soon reach our destination. There is no road too long, there is no price too high and there is no time too far for the person who advances deliberately and without undue hesitation. Your day will come! Your time will arrive without fail! However, it is a matter of waiting patiently.

The Fruits of Waiting

Sometimes, it looks as if your turn will never come. You see your mates making it in life, and you wonder where you are getting it wrong. Sometimes you get tired of waiting for your time to shine despite all the efforts you have put in place. I have been there before. Many years ago, as a young man in the church, I used to have lots of revelations and deep insights about some scriptures. I longed to be given the pulpit to preach. I practised my preaching in the open field and in front of the mirror without an audience. Nobody saw any form of greatness and the "x-factor" in me as a preacher. A lot of times, I had loads of messages that I yearned for the chance to show my preaching prowess. Those times were quite frustrating. And unfortunately, the opportunity to preach never came.

It took a long time for my turn to come. But during the silent period of no activity, God groomed my ability to wait. Waiting means doing nothing for a period until something happens. It is a period where you are expecting something to happen. It is being on the lookout for the actualisation of the purpose of God. God often delays the answers to our prayers to teach us the virtue of patience. Waiting is not a passive attitude towards what is required of us in life. It means taking time to produce a life of quality.

Below are some of the attributes waiting develops in you:

1. Patience

Your patience will achieve more than your impatience. It serves as a protection against wrongs as clothes protect humans from cold. If you put on more clothes as the cold increases, the cold will have no power to hurt you. Similarly, we must grow in patience when we encounter challenging situations, and they will be too powerless to vex our minds.

2. Rest
Rest is not idleness or indolence. To lie sometimes on the grass on a summer day listening to the murmur of water, or watching the clouds float across the sky, is hardly a waste of time. We all need to spend time adoring the beauty of nature around us. Learn to rest your mind and your heart.

3. Assurance
This is to enable us to regain confidence, strength and resilience, not in ourselves but in God and His ability. This recharges and refuels our spiritual reserves. What matters is not the idea a man holds but the depth at which he holds it. Thus, waiting creates assurance, belief and conviction.

4. Submission
Waiting tunes our hearts to God's feelings. This enables us to spend quality time with Him and experience His glory. We cannot fulfil God's

purposes for our lives while focusing on our plans. The degree of blessing enjoyed by any man corresponds with the completeness of God's victory over him.

5. Transformation

Waiting on God transforms us from self into God-centeredness. Waiting prepares us for God to manifest Himself in us and through us. It empties us of ourselves and prepares us for God. Isolation often models you after your assignment in life.

6. Faith

Spending time with God activates faith, boldness and courage. A step of faith in His presence can make you do the impossible. God did not promise us days without pain, laughter without sorrow, or sun without rain, but He did promise strength for the day, comfort for the tears, and light for the way. If God brings you to it, He will bring you through it. Faith is not the ability to believe long and far into the mist future. It is simply taking God at His Word as we take the next step.

7. Power

We walk in great power, anointing and supernatural authority when we wait on God. Nothing tries our faith like waiting on God for answers to prayers. It will test our submission to Him as our trustworthy authority. Waiting is not necessarily resignation from all activity; it is submission to God's better idea. It means that our life is brought under God's umbrella of authority and direction.

Timing is Everything

In life, we are always waiting for something. We wait for a dream to come to pass. We wait for the right person, and we also wait for a problem to turn around. And when it does not happen as fast as we want, we get frustrated and discouraged. However, you have to realise that the moment we pray, God establishes a set time to answer. There is a moment designated for everything we will ever pray for and ask God for. As written in Psalm 102:13 (AMP), *"You will arise and have mercy and loving-kindness for Zion, for it is time to have pity and compassion for her; yes, the set time has come [the moment designated]."*

God has a set time for you to meet the right person; there is also a set time for your problems to turn around. There is a set time for your healing, promotion, breakthrough and for your ministry to come to full maturity. It may be tomorrow, next week or five years from now. Nevertheless, when you understand the time has already been set, it takes all the pressure off. You will no longer be worried, wondering when you would relax and enjoy your life, knowing that God has scheduled the promise. Whether you are a young minister, servant, associate pastor, church elder, church leader, departmental head or a long-standing member of any organisation, there is a fixed time for your inauguration.

In the words of Robert H. Schuller, "Never cut a tree down in the wintertime. Never make a negative decision in the low time. Never make your most important decisions when you are in your worst moods. Wait. Be patient. The storm will pass. Spring will come." The waiting period is a test of your talent and ability, so wait for your turn to come. In the moment of waiting, you may be isolated or abandoned, but you should never despise the days of small beginnings. Anyone can count the seeds in an apple, but only God can count the number of apples in a seed. God's delay is not His denial. Your time will definitely come.

WHY ISOLATION?

Success consists of going from failure to failure without loss of enthusiasm
- Winston Churchill

Why does God put us in isolation? Isolation is not intended to be a place of our humiliation but a place of preparation. Greatness is in the preparation, not in the performance. God often incubates a gift (or a talent, a dream and a mission) before revealing it to the world. You are where you are today because there is a set time for your manifestation. You may feel excluded, disqualified, ineligible and disabled, but God deploys the underdogs to confront the giants. Our gifts and talents are prepared in isolation, and great callings are often hidden so as to fully mature. We learn more in our valley experiences than on our mountaintops. And whether we like it or not, every one of us regardless of age, gender, position, nationality, economic status, race, or religious background will be thrown into some kind of a valley of loneliness.

Why do we prepare great men and women in secret? Why do doctors, sportsmen, athletes, actors, and special forces prepare in secret? The time in isolation is crucial to greatness. All through history, things have been done behind the scenes. You are no different. Perhaps you are wondering why nobody is celebrating you. Why aren't you given the chance to do what you see as glamorous, prestigious and prominent? It's because isolation creates a product. Every scene of your life has some part to play in the final product.

Let's examine Exodus 3:1-3 — *Now Moses kept the flock of Jethro, his father-in-law, the priest of Midian: and he led the flock to the backside of the desert, and came to the mountain of God, even to Horeb. And the angel of the LORD appeared unto him in a flame of fire out of the midst of a bush: and he looked, and, behold, the bush burned with fire, and the bush was not consumed. And Moses said, I will now turn aside, and see this great sight, why the bush is not burnt.*

Why the backside of the desert? Moses was kept at the backside because of the product he carried. Young David did not take care of his father's flock alone because he was a lost cause in society; rather, it was due to his ordained assignment. You may have wondered when your time would come. When are you also going to be called upon like that gifted preacher, young and successful entrepreneur, great coach or excellent singer? Always remember that you are in isolation because of the product you carry. Isolation can be one of the darkest valleys of life. Valleys are surrounded by hills. Keep looking up; soon your daydreaming will become a reality. Every great accomplishment is brought into manifestation by holding on to the vision, and oftentimes before the big achievement, failure and discouragement will come in multiple folds.

Why do we go through the darkest valleys of life?

When we are in isolation, we recover the treasures of life. Wherever we stumble lies our treasure. Life is a succession of lessons, stages and scenes that must be lived to be understood. All great innovations were built in isolation. You are a great invention in the making. Keep going through your period of isolation. Remember, quality is built with time, not in a hurry.

Let us look at some of the reasons we go through isolation in life.

1. Isolation is a Passageway Rather Than a Destination.

The backside of the desert is a passageway, not a destination. There were times in my life, ministry and family when it looked like we were finished. The verdict had been passed. The conclusion had been drawn. It seemed as if we would fail and would never amount to anything. However, I saw it as a passage. A passage is like a channel; it is a route and a voyage. Life is towards a destination. Because I endured those nights of pain, isolation and loneliness, I am qualified to tell you that you aren't going to die or be frozen in oblivion. You are on a passageway to something big. The greater the glory, the greater the pain. No lasting glory is won without struggles.

A victory without war is a compromise. If you are a star without a scar, you are just a pretender. Great generals have moments when they thought they would die. But they kept fighting and in the end, they have medals to prove it. You must understand that isolation is just a passageway to your destination. In an airport, you will see all kinds of aircrafts. Some would take off, go round the city and return to port. Some taxi around and are brought back to base. Some are also grounded; they are going nowhere. Yet, there is a category that takes off and heads towards a destination. In life, you are also heading towards a destination. Many of life's failures are people who did not realise how close they were to success when they gave up in isolation.

2. God Controls the Depth and the Length of our Valley Experience

Safety comes in our proximity to God, not in our distance from our enemies. Nothing happens to a child of God without a warrant from heaven. There has never been a time in your life that something happened to you or your family without God's approval. Have you realised that your teacher is always silent when you are taking a test? It's a sign of confidence in your ability. God will not allow anything to happen to you, your family and your vision if He has not adequately prepared you for it. 1 Corinthians 10:13 tells us that *"There hath no temptation taken you but such as is common to man: but God is faithful, who will not suffer you to be tempted above that ye are able; but will with the temptation also make a way to escape, that ye may be able to bear it."*

God does not remove us from all harm because He uses harm to move us close to Him. There has never been a time in life that God allowed something beyond your strength to happen to you. Every one of life's tragedies is a strategy to bring you to a place of accomplishment. God does not do accidents, mishaps and mistakes. You are in isolation because of what you carry. The story of Job in the Bible proves that nothing happens to us without God's concern.

According to Job 1:8-11, *"And the LORD said unto Satan, Hast thou considered my servant Job, that there is none like him in the earth, a perfect and an upright man, one that feared God, and escheweth evil? Then Satan answered the LORD, and said, Doth Job fear God for nought? Hast not thou made a hedge about him, and about his house, and about all that he hath on every side? thou hast blessed the work of his hands, and his substance is increased in the land. But put forth thine hand now, and touch all that he hath, and he will curse thee to thy face."*

From the passage above, you would see that it

was God who posed the question. No one but the tutor decides the test after the lesson. God controls the depth and the length of your valley experience. Nothing just happens! Our "safe place" is not where we live; it is in whom we live. God may not always come immediately you call Him, but He is always on time. Never forget that God controls what happens in your life.

3. The Deeper the Valley, the Greater the Work God Will do Through us

It always amazes me when I think of the fact that every house on every street is full of many stories. Similarly, every pew in our churches is full of many triumphs and tragedies, but all we see are yards, driveways and nice clothing. Many of the people we celebrate in our generation today have the greatest scars and disfigurations. The deeper your isolation, the greater the work God wants to do in your life.

Jesus had to wait for thirty years before commencing the greatest work on earth — redemption. Moses had to wait for forty years to lead the Israelites out of Egypt into freedom. Your longevity in life is relatively proportional to your preparation. Shallow preparation precedes disaster.

And a spectacular achievement is always preceded by unspectacular preparation. Success means having the courage, determination, and will to become the person you believe you were meant to be. However, it will take long and extended hours of preparation. The difference between you and any successful person in life is preparation.

This present generation can easily buy success, greatness and accomplishment. There is nothing like timing and patience. The greatest and long-lasting edifices we see today have great foundations. The higher the building, the deeper the foundation. Strong structures require a solid foundation. We have too many quitters and complainers. Many want greatness but detest the price for greatness. They are wishful thinkers who will never amount to anything. The glory is in correlation to the pain. If we study the lives of great men and women carefully, we will find that their greatness was developed through the darker periods of their lives. One of the largest tributaries of the river of greatness is the stream of adversity.

4. We learn more in a valley experience than we do on the mountaintop of life.

There is something beautiful about scars. A scar

means the hurt is over, the wound is closed and healed. You are the most valuable asset in your journey to the top. In life, we do not learn much in a crowd; we learn most when we are alone. The greatest lesson of my life came when I was alone and isolated. I later realised that God was up to something in my life all along. Perhaps you feel low and disconnected. But you know what? The class is on; you are in an academic session, and the tutor is the Holy Spirit. Other tutors include leaders and the people who put you through the most traumatic experiences in life. They bring the best out of you.

Joseph went through a lot in the hands of his own brothers. They disowned him and sold him to slavery. They even wanted him dead. He went through the pain of being dragged to a foreign land, the pain of disconnection from his family and home. Against his will, he embarked on the loneliest journey one could ever make and the mental battering of the unknown. He was wrongly accused by Potiphar's wife and his fellow friends in prison had a change of fortune before him. But in all of these, he was not discouraged.

These experiences turned him into the Jesus of the Old Testament. Hebrew 12:2-3 reads: *"Looking unto Jesus the author and finisher of our faith; who for the joy that was set before him endured the cross, despising the shame, and is set down at the right hand of the throne of God. For consider him that endured such contradiction of sinners against himself, lest ye be wearied and faint in your minds."*

Joseph had learnt so much through the darkest moment of the valley experience. The whole idea of his ascension was because of the product he carried. The famous statement everybody quotes in Genesis 50:20 was borne out of adversity and isolation. *"But as for you, ye thought evil against me; but God meant it unto good, to bring to pass, as it is this day, to save much people alive."* When you go through challenges, you turn out to be an inspiration. You become an institution people learn from.

Never label anything you never worked or fought for and probably learn from as a legacy or a success. Life is a big classroom with invisible classmates and tutors. Don't think of the cost. Think of the value. No matter how many mistakes you make or how slow your progress is, you are still way ahead of someone who isn't trying.

5. Isolation is Designed to Bring the Best out of You.

Isolation helps us to uncover character strengths and virtues that may not have been apparent. It brings out the best in people. It also helps us to slow down, take stock, and reevaluate our lives. I taught my daughter how to ride a bicycle. Many times, when we went to the field with lots of people watching her, she would fall off the bicycle. She often felt embarrassed afterwards. The day I taught her in isolation without the gaze of people, learning came easily. In isolation, the best in you is perfected. When people hear me speak and preach, they often tell me, "I love the way you preach". Some church members even beg me to preach every Sunday in our church. I have people who have fallen in love with my ministry because of my style of preaching. What these people don't know is that I was once a church boy who was never allowed to preach or stand in front of any group.

After my first preaching engagement at a Scripture Union programme, a group of girls mocked me. There was a particular American jargon I liked to use in those days. Instead of saying "we are going to", I would say "you gonna". These topset girls counted each time I used the phrase, which was more than a hundred and fifty times. After the meeting, everybody began calling me "you gonna". It was embarrassing and awkward. It knocked the confidence out of me. Afterwards, I felt frightened whenever I was called to speak.

I took to the hills and woods in my town with my script and my preaching. I preached to trees and grasses and whatever was in my way until I ran out of breath, strength and energy. I got tired of the repetition and loneliness, so I walked back home, alone. But I knew I carried a special gift; I knew I had a powerful insight into the word of God. Although nobody would hear me preach or teach in public, the product was perfected and refined in isolation. This is what my admirers don't know today.

There's something you are doing now that will take you to the top. There's an assignment your senior pastor or your boss has given you that is not glamorous and attractive. But if you will work hard to perfect the product, your time will come. Many of the outstanding presentations and talents you admire were produced in isolation. Nobody can go back and start a new beginning, but anyone can start today and make a new ending. You can decide how it ends today.

6. Isolation is not the Problem but the Product You Carry.

Your talent is God's gift to you, but what you do with it is your gift to God. There are many gifted people who haven't fulfilled their dreams because they were too cautious and were unwilling to take the leap of faith. I know some talented people who have wasted their lives; they never arrived at their destined place because they could not stand alone. The type of battle you face in life determines the kind of victory you win. The challenges you face are a clue to the strengths you have been endowed with. Everything we face in life is also a measurement of the product we carry.

The people who face no problems, fight no battles, overcome no barriers, face no opposition, and have no challenges to resolve are living in the graveyard. As long as you have a gift, a ministry, a dream and an assignment, you will have confrontations with tragedies in life. The intensity of the heat depends on how much the furnace fire you can carry. In schools, students are tested based on their ability, not their availability. Your test is dependent on the product you are designed to be. You cannot heat cast iron and plywood together. You cannot compare your predicament to somebody else's. Your dilemma and the vicious cycle of life are designed to precipitate a certain response due to what you carry. You are engineered for something great in life. Therefore, your challenges will vary.

7. Isolation Builds Your Tenacity.

Tenacity requires staying in the game no matter what kind of valley we encounter in life. Have tenacity. Decide what you want the outcome to be then, change and evolve. Create an improved product. It is not about how hard you can hit; it's about how hard you can get hit as well as how much you can take and keep moving forward. Being tenacious means you are willing to stick firmly to a decision, plan, or opinion without changing or doubting it. In isolation, tenacity is born. Lots of quitters succeed in the limelight and public eye. But many winners and champions succeed in isolation. The difference between winners and quitters is tenacity. How much do you really want that dream? How far can you go? How much can you take? Listen to all the inventors of our generation; they spent nights and burnt the midnight oil alone to make a series of progress that accumulated to success. Isolation is a city called ten-a-city.

Why do sports men and women go to camps to prepare for tournaments? Why would a heavyweight champion still pitch a camp to train for his next fight? Why did Usain Bolt, the world 100-metre record holder, pitch a camp outside his comfortable and luxurious home to train? These men and women spend time in isolation to build tenacity. Normally, we see abandonment as some form of weapon to destroy us. David could kill Goliath because his wilderness experience had trained him. Overcoming Goliath was like a replay of the template of what took place in the backside of the wilderness. Wear your wilderness experience like a wristwatch, and do not pull it out just to show that you have one. But remember you have it.

8. Isolation Allows God to Examine What is in Your Heart.

God will often examine your intention in order to select His interventions. Some so-called disappointed men and women of God may not amount to anything in life because they have the wrong intentions. Whenever I meet young pastors who like to complain about their superiors, I immediately know why they aren't going to make it. Of course, I am no judge or God. The moments you feel frustrated and upset often expose the real intent and content of your heart.

When Elijah conquered the prophets of Baal and fled from Jezebel, he alighted at Beersheba and sat down under a juniper tree, and he prayed that God should take away his life. *"And Ahab told Jezebel all that Elijah had done, and withal how he had slain all the prophets with the sword. Then Jezebel sent a messenger unto Elijah, saying, So let the gods do to me, and more also, if I make not thy life as the life of one of them by tomorrow about this time. And when he saw that, he arose, and went for his life, and came to Beersheba, which belongeth to Judah, and left his servant there. But he himself went a day's journey into the wilderness, and came and sat down under a juniper tree: and he requested for himself that he might die; and said, It is enough; now, O LORD, take away my life; for I am not better than my fathers."* (1 Kings 19:1-4)

The prophet who had slain about four hundred and fifty Baal worshipers felt isolated, so he sought death. When you are at your wit's end and you feel cornered or beaten into oblivion, what is in you will puff out. Isolation has a way of unearthing the contents of one's heart. There is a moment in everybody's life when you will find yourself in an isolated place. It's like being in the winepress, where you will be squeezed into a tight place, and the content in your heart will erupt. For many, this content normally detonates when they least expect. Lots of people have had the shock of their lives when they fell into tight places. The story of a man is never complete until he has passed through a tight place in life. When reality hits you and you are pushed to the edge, whatever is in your heart is bound to come out. The content of a man's heart will be examined when he finds himself in isolation.

There is a day when we will be examined not by an examination board or a panel of judges but by a place in life called isolation. This is where our true and hidden motives are laid bare. Isolation often uncovers hidden and concealed motivations. What drives you is not discovered until you are in solitary confinement.

INFORMATION

Information is an investment for superior participation in life.

Information is power, and it is valuable because it affects behaviours, decisions and outcomes. When you have information on what others do not have, it gives you the upper hand in that field of endeavour. In the place of isolation, we should go for information. You should understand that God teaches you in the place of isolation. When you miss the essence of a thing, abuse is inevitable. Some people think they are being punished in the place of isolation. But I have learnt to never see a lack of activity as a wasted period. When you do not hear from God, it does not mean he is not speaking.

Let's explore Exodus 3:1, which says *"Now Moses kept the flock of Jethro, his father-in-law, the priest of Midian: and he led the flock to the backside of the desert, and came to the mountain of God, even to Horeb."*

Moses kept the flock of His father-in-law at the backside of the desert for forty years. What exactly was he doing? What was the schedule? What was going on for those forty years? Something must be happening. Isolation can be either your prison or your palace. What you make of it is your decision. Life has its woes, so learn to be on your toes. Be on the alert at all times. People might see isolation as an exclusion, but I chose to see mine as an incision.

When Moses was isolated to the backside of the desert, it was a class above any human institution. If you are going to lead people out of slavery and write the first five books of the Torah, you do not need to go to Harvard, Oxford, Eaton, Cambridge, or Yale. What you need is God's school of tuition. In God's university, he isolates you in order to integrate you. God will often train us in the most unlikely places on earth for His glory.

All the time that David was alone there in the wilderness, he was gathering intelligence. He was adequately equipping himself for a moment in his life that would turn his destiny around. God has a way of taking flawed materials and making a king out of them. Never underestimate the place of isolation. I see it as a place of divine learning, where you receive first-hand information. When you are alone, you are in the best place of information. This current generation is in a hurry. Many people are half-baked and underdeveloped, yet they aspire to get to the top. The top requires information. And if you are not adequately informed in life, you will be deformed. The premature collapse of great visions, dreams, marriages and even gifts is because of a lack of adequate information.

Fast Food Generation

By failing to prepare, we are preparing to fail. We live in a fast and swift generation. We are accustomed to fast food and microwaved meals. Although these means of preparing meals are not wrong, we call them junk food and we frown upon them. Why? Because it is not good for our health. We have worse health problems in this generation than in any other generation. Our physical health is poor, our mental health is degenerating, our families are disintegrating and our world is going crazy. Why is our world falling apart? Why are our children vulnerable and exposed to dangers in the comfort of their homes? Why are there so many casualties in politics and failed leaders? We live in a fast lane generation that does not take time to harness gifts, ministries, talents and missions. We want things done quickly.

But then, there is no time to waste in life, and there is no cut and paste here. Champions do not become champions when they win the event, but in the hours, weeks, months and years they spend preparing in isolation. The victorious performance is merely the demonstration of their championship character, spirit, and disposition. Dreams do not become a reality through magic; it takes prayer, determination, and hard work in isolation. Never waste your time doing nothing. Life is approached in two ways — a holiday retreat or a boot camp. We were never born with a silver spoon in our mouths. We were born with a diamond spoon in our palms. Carry it by yourself, and work on it. Nothing happens by chance. If nobody knows you or celebrates you today, it is not a curse. You are not a failure; you are simply in isolation. And your best will soon come forth. Your season of greatness will come if you do not despair.

Moses spent forty years in Egypt. He spent another forty years in the wilderness, looking after sheep and cows. Eighty years of preparation is enough to drain a man's hope, faith and confidence. When God called him, he said he could not speak. Yet he was one of the greatest thinkers of his generation. Moses is one of the greatest authors that ever lived. How did he know the story of creation? Why was he able to tell the story of Adam, Eve, Noah as well as the creative and formative years of the earth? In the place of isolation, a divine download takes place. You know something you cannot explain. This is called a revelation. And a revelation is a knowledge inspired and revealed by the Holy Spirit.

There is an impartation of knowledge when you are in isolation. We cannot hurry our generals; we can only hope that they come through the war and receive their medals. Many gifted people are wasting their time looking for glamour. They have refused to spend time in isolation to develop their gifts and sharpen their skills. If you want to go to the top, stay and survive at the top, what you are doing now will determine your chances of survival. Moses spent eighty years in obscurity; meanwhile, he was being built for security. You may be in an obscure part of the earth today. Yet you may be carrying one of the greatest, most profound and insightful assignments on earth. Your obscurity is not a punishment but a platform for preparation.

Information Affects Our Behaviour

Information breeds transformation. The number one value of the 21st century is the influx of information. It is a privilege to be alive in this generation. We are inundated with technology and information. A lot of us have been schooled, but not all of us have been educated. Make no mistake; it is great to go to university and college. But the fact that you have a degree from an accredited university does not make you educated. Any man who spends time in isolation with the intention of learning has an advantage over others in life.

Today, the world is a global village because of shared information. Information affects our behaviour; it activates renovation, reformation and reconstruction. It will activate your performance and your manners. People are not lethargic; they simply have impotent goals — goals that do not inspire them or anybody around them. When you spend time alone with God in isolation, God will inspire you to know things that took others a long time to know. The world we live in has changed so much because of information. Invest in information. While your time has not come, invest in yourself. Learn something new every day. Never see your fallow period as a time-wasted venture. It is a calculated plan of God to create a masterpiece of an institution in our generation.

Proverbs 23:23 urges us to *"Buy the truth, and sell it not; also wisdom, and instruction, and understanding."* Information is an investment for a superior participation in life. We are a generation that is so blessed with information technology. We study new things in our schools and try to be abreast with the times we live in. Yet there are a number of people who will not seek information. I am a preacher, hence I speak to all kinds of people. For me to make the maximum impact I was called to make, I need to be adequately equipped for superior participation. We have a new breed of a generation coming up. They are high-tech in their dealings. Their level of communication has never been seen before, and we need a new breed of preachers, youth leaders and managers.

Information Can Replace Systems

What is a system? A system is a set of things working together as parts of a mechanism or an interconnecting network, a complex whole, association and linkage. A system can also be a way of thinking. If you want to change the way people do certain things, change the information they carry. In life, if your system and fundamental beliefs are compromised, your structure will eventually crumble. The strength of every system is based on the pillars on which it is built. In the world we live in today, we need men and women with proven lives to change the way the next generation thinks. We need gifted people who are not confined to a certain way of life due to their lack of information. Whenever God wants to use a person, he throws them into oblivion. It is a place of absolute silence. Everybody who wants to move to the top needs obscurity to stand the test of light. In that place of nothingness, you build yourself for the challenges ahead.

Information Gives You Leverage In Life

The wealthiest person today is not somebody with tons of gold or a safe full of pounds or dollars. It is somebody who has information. I pastor a church full of black ethnic minorities in the UK. Our greatest challenge is how to buy the truth. If you have information, you have influence in life.

In Proverbs 23:23, we were told to buy the truth, and sell it not; also, wisdom, and instruction, and understanding. The Hebrew word for buy is "qanah" which means to erect, to create, and to procure especially by purchase. The onus is on us to erect, which means to assemble, build and construct information. I decided to write volume two of Moving To The Top to encourage people who are serving in great institutions that their time will come. Many are campaigning to be given an opportunity to show their talents. They must buy the truth and invest in themselves. Their day will definitely come.

As a pastor of a local church, I would like to share a few of my experiences with you. I had a gentleman in our church one time. He wanted to preach so badly. He told me he was ready, and sometimes I had a chat with him and saw that he was not ready. I told him to get some of my tapes and CDs to learn presentations and how to deliver sermons. He told me he was led by the spirit and did not need any help.

On a set date, which I had given him four months earlier, I told him he would share an exhortation in church. He was delighted about the opportunity. Well, this gentleman had the call of God. He spoke and dressed well, had a degree and lived in a great neighbourhood. He spoke in tongues, and he was a dedicated chap. I told him he would do a ten-minute exhortation, but he said he needed more than that. So, I gave him the full length of my preaching time, which is about fifty-five minutes. I introduced him during the particular Sunday service. I want you to picture a wonderfully dressed gentleman with his folder and a massive Bible mounting the podium. But six minutes into his sermon, he was repeating himself. It seemed the eager brother had lost all the words he wanted to use. That is the evidence of lack of isolation. Before that day, I had advised him to buy information, but he refused. Hone your skills today because you might be called forward to demonstrate your skills tomorrow.

Wherever you are at the moment is not a time to be lazy. Buy the truth, invest in yourself, and read a book a week. Learn to communicate. Many marriages end in divorce because instead of studying and learning what marriage is, we spiritualise marriage and eventually, it fails. The gentleman I told you about had everything going for him. The only thing he lacked was understanding of his time alone with God. When you invest in yourself, you become an investment for your generation. The race is for those who have invested, not for those who are only interested. Life is about transformation, and information activates transformation. Your greatest asset in life is not your money, marriage, or membership but your memory bank. How rich are you in your field of endeavour? What are you doing now that nobody knows you? What would you change if you were given the time to start again? It is never too late to start again. Don't let what you don't have stop you from getting what you could have.

Everything we know today are products of learning. Nobody was ever born disabled. You may be physically unable, but you are not disabled. You can become whatever you want to be if you will spend time developing yourself in isolation. It is not so bad if nobody buys your books or CDs today. The good news is you still have time to improve yourself. Get the information you need, and make yourself better. Where there is a carcass, the vultures will gather. Therefore, my dearly beloved friend, isolation is a place of information. Information — either spiritual or natural — will give you power, influence, and leverage in life.

The next chapter will examine skills. In isolation, you don't just buy information, but you develop the skills, talent and the ability that will take you to the top.

SKILL

*Every great person in any field of life
was first an amateur.*

Education is not a pile of information, data and facts; rather, it is an unveiling of hidden talents and a seed of greatness. We are living in a fast-moving generation; everything seems to be going at a supersonic speed. In view of the dynamics of our generation, we seem to be in a hurry. We fast-track our doctors, teachers, nurses and even our police officers. The rush, therefore, gives rise to half-baked and half-fried professionals. We even have graduates who are still illiterates. The irony is that hanging your degree certificate on your office wall does not give you experience or make you skillful. You must develop your latent gifts and talents.

J. K. Rowling wrote Harry Potter and became a household name. Rowling was working as a researcher and bilingual secretary for Amnesty International when she conceived the idea for the Harry Potter series on a delayed train from Manchester to London in 1990. The seven-year period that followed saw the death of her mother, divorce from her first husband and relative poverty until she finished the first novel in the series in 1997. Before she was ushered to the spotlight, the seed of greatness had always been in her. She had to work as a secretary and perhaps develop her skills over the years.

You also have a potential, but God will not bring you to the fore until you are ready and until you have sharpened your skills. What is a skill? It is the ability to do something well. It connotes expertise, competence, proficiency and experience. In the place of isolation, development of skill and experience takes place. Never assume greatness in any field if you have not developed in that area.

In numerous instances, the Bible stresses the importance of personal development. Apostle

Paul in 1 Timothy 3:1-6 said, *"This is a true saying, if a man desires the office of a bishop, he desireth a good work. A bishop then must be blameless, the husband of one wife, vigilant, sober, of good behaviour, given to hospitality, apt to teach; Not given to wine, no striker, not greedy of filthy lucre; but patient, not a brawler, not covetous; One that ruleth well his own house, having his children in subjection with all gravity; For if a man know not how to rule his own house, how shall he take care of the church of God? Not a novice, lest being lifted up with pride he falls into the condemnation of the devil."*

The passage above uncovers a model for bishops and church leaders. In verse six, Apostle Paul emphasised that whoever will lead God's people must not be a novice. Unfortunately, the church of God is now filled with many self-proclaimed pastors who know nothing about the ministry. They only seek to gratify their selfish interests. We even have successful people with no experience, skills or competence because their success is built on compromise. One of the truest tests of integrity is the blunt refusal to be compromised.

Sometimes back, I took my little son for football practice, and there was an ongoing session. And he seemed to wonder why we couldn't go in to play as soon as we arrived. This session is called skill practice where the coach or trainer takes them through a particular skill. As I watched on the sidelines, I noticed that some of the children were talented. Yet they went through about half an hour of skill practice. Why did they have to practise? No matter the amount of talent you have, practice makes you perfect. These series of practice will harmonise your skills. Skill development does not happen by accident; it takes dedication and conscious efforts.

There are many gifted people from the developing world. But we may not have heard of them because their opportunity has not yet come. What if their greatest opportunity comes and they have no skills? Some people, like I do, believe that a supernatural door will open to us one day. However, if this door swings open and we have not learnt how to handle it, then we are not ready. Now that you are still in obscurity, spend quality time to enrich and deepen your God-given talent. God has given you all you need to create what you want in life, but the onus is on you to identify and work on it.

The Essentials of Skills Practice

The greatest part of the football session I mentioned earlier was the skills practice. We were once invited for the Talent Identification Programme Session (TIPS). In TIPS, talented and prospective footballers are identified subsequently and trained. From the session, I learnt that no man is born without a talent or a gift. What we normally fail to do is to develop it.

My greatest worry, as a pastor responsible for lives and gifts development, is that many gifted people fizzle in the face of opportunity. I realised in my teenage years that I might be called to preach the greatest message to humanity. Born and bred in Ghana, English is our national language but my second language. I sold newspapers for the majority of my teenage years and used the opportunity to cultivate the habit of reading and improve my language skills. So, gifts alone may not be enough, and opportunity alone may not cut it for you. Lobbying may get you to some places in life, but developing your skills and talents will keep your doors of opportunities from curving in.

Here are a few tips to consider if you want to develop skill in your area of assignment:

1. One Skill at a Time

One skill at a time is the best shot to greatness. Whether you are a pastor, a leader or a parent, you need to cultivate the right skills to get to the pinnacle of success you desire. In the football sessions I attend with my son, I am always amazed at the patience of the coaches and trainers. Have you ever asked yourself why footballers have coaches or why do boxers train in the gym? Also, why should pilots go for training every now and then? These professionals need to practise and acquire new skills for new challenges. It is all about developing their skills.

Today's greatest skill may not be enough for tomorrow's challenges. You may be great at what you do today, but skills development will keep you at the cutting-edge of life. Regardless of your field of endeavour, one skill at a time will see you at the top. The story of David and Goliath often amazes me, particularly how a lad managed to overpower a giant. David learnt to use what he had to get what he wanted. A would-be king of Israel spent his adolescent life looking after sheep.

> *"And Saul said to David, You are not able to go to fight against this Philistine. You*

are only an adolescent, and he has been a warrior from his youth. And David said to Saul, Your servant kept his father's sheep. And when there came a lion or again a bear and took a lamb out of the flock. I went out after it and smote it and delivered the lamb out of its mouth; and when it arose against me, I caught it by its beard and smote it and killed it. Your servant killed both the lion and the bear; and this uncircumcised Philistine shall be like one of them, for he has defied the armies of the living God!" **1 Samuel 17:34-36 (AMP)**

The boldness with which he confronted Goliath showed that he was prepared. He was not caught unawares because he had earlier killed a lion and a bear while in the wilderness — preparation. As you are waiting for the right opportunity, what skills do you have? At the backside of the wilderness where nobody knows you, what are you doing? If David had been idle, he would never have summoned the courage to face Goliath. In fact, King Saul never doubted David's boldness, but he doubted his skill. Goliath had been a warrior from his youth and being a giant, Saul thought none among the Israelites could confront him. This is why it is important for you to cultivate your skills. The book of Judges talked about a group of people who were left-handed. They could sling stones at the width of the human hair without missing (Judges 20:16). This means that what David did was not a prank but a product of skills. It must have been a common weapon carried by shepherds for protection, but he mastered it. What if he had been idle before Goliath showed up? The story would have been different today. In the same manner, develop your skills so that when an opportunity presents itself, you will act with confidence.

2. Repeated Actions Are Rewarded

Just as an athlete who practices constantly is rewarded with success, repeated actions in life are often rewarded with either positive or negative reports. David had killed a bear and a lion with his bare hands, so he knew he could get to the top with a bit of practice. What made him believe he could kill Goliath was not his height, stature, physique or reputation but his testimony. He knew that repetition is rewarding.

Many people give up too soon because they feel like they are repeating actions without seeing results. Of course, there are things that we do not need to repeat in life. But sometimes in developing a skill, you need a repetitive attitude. Nobody succeeds without repeating certain patterns. David said a lion and a bear attacked the flock, and he slew them. Nobody knew about those gallant acts, but he knew that everything is possible with skills. He walked into the palace to confront the giant as a repetition of his audacious skill. What differentiates outstanding people from average people is their ability to hone their skill. You become what you constantly do. If you practise excellence, you become excellent. If you practise laziness, you become lazy. Whatever you repeat in life determines your reward.

As of the time I was writing this book, my first daughter was learning how to play the keyboard. Sometimes, I got worried because she spent little time on the keyboard. But I knew she must want the skill so much that she would be willing to spend time with it. Then I met another girl just about the same age as my daughter who did not start playing as early as my daughter did. I realised she was more competent than my daughter because of the repetition of actions. What will get you to the place of fulfilment is skills, not talent, money or opulence. And any good skill you repeat will be rewarded.

3. What You Know Today May Not be Relevant Tomorrow.

The skills that got you out of Egypt are not the same skills that will get you to the Promised Land. The knowledge you acquire today may not be relevant tomorrow. Because of the present inflow of information, what we know in five years will take the previous generation more years. As soon as the Israelites got to the Promised Land, the manna ceased. God gave them corn instead, which means a new level requires a new measure.

> *"And the manna ceased on the morrow after they had eaten of the old corn of the land; neither had the children of Israel manna anymore, but they did eat of the fruit of the land of Canaan that year."*
> **Joshua 5:12**

With the presence of the corn, they had to learn to farm, plough the land, sow the seed and harvest it. Above all, they learnt to turn the corn into whatever they wanted. This required skills. In Egypt, all they did was build houses and look after themselves. But in the Promised Land, they had to learn new skills to live by themselves. The skills of yesteryears may not be suitable for the next phase of your journey. The truest sense of greatness is not fame but the ability to outlive your past. Governing a shop requires skills, not strength. In the place of isolation, God wants you to be stretched so you can last. Do not write books that nobody wants to read after it is launched. Do not invent a product that dies with you. We live in a world that evolves every day, and we must do all we can to stay relevant.

4. Communicate What You Are Called to do Skilfully

Good and clear communication skills are one of the essential management skills everyone needs. Talent and gift alone are not enough. We should be able to communicate skillfully. Communication is the process of exchanging information, ideas, thoughts, feelings and emotions through speech, signals, writing, or behaviour. Many would-be leaders have melted into oblivion because they couldn't communicate their gifts and talents skillfully. Where I was born, there were no formal or informal manuals for raising leaders. It was more of observational and oral learning. What we observed in our parents, teachers and mentors constituted what we know.

To get to the top, we must acquire the right skills. Different levels of challenges demand different skills. Although I did not have the privilege to have been born in the developed world, I acquired skills in the place of isolation. I developed the habit of learning something new every day. Many of the younger generation lack work ethics and consistency. They also lack the desire to be the best in everything they do. It is not enough to be gifted; you must skill up.

When David went to the Valley of Elah to give his brothers food as instructed by his father, one of his elder brothers, Eliab, tried to bully him. The manner in which he spoke to David was enough to send him running back to the wilderness. But he was not bothered. He gathered information about what would be done to whomever conquered Goliath. 1 Samuel 17:28-30 noted that *"And Eliab his eldest brother heard when he spake unto the men; and Eliab's anger was kindled against David, and he said, Why camest thou down hither? and with whom hast thou left those few sheep in the wilderness? I know thy pride, and the naughtiness of thine heart; for thou art come down that thou mightest see the battle. And David said, What have I now done? Is there not a cause? And he turned from him toward another, and spake after the same manner: and the people answered him again after the former manner."*

Over the years, David had mastered the skill of communicating his ability. He never sold himself short. He had the talent but needed to communicate it skillfully when his brother said, "I know thy pride, and the naughtiness of thine heart." Perhaps his family had noticed his intelligence. His father sent him all alone to the battlefield though their nation was under terrorists' attack. A Chinese proverb says, "Teachers open the doors, but you must enter by yourself." Here was a lad who thought his time would never come. He was probably never called to family gatherings due to his pride and naughtiness of heart.

Then one afternoon, he came in contact with what he was destined for — to fight and conquer Goliath. What if after seeing that opportunity he could not communicate skilfully? David's private practice gave him an opportunity for a skillful performance. What if God has really answered your prayer but you couldn't handle the pressure of the big brother? What if as a gifted lead singer you fumbled when you had an opportunity to display your skills? To prevent these avoidable situations, cultivate life skills. Skills don't just fly in as soon as you hit the mayday button; instead, you develop your skills deliberately.

David was born to kill Goliath, but he needed to learn how to communicate skilfully. The King tried to talk him out of it, but he responded in a manner that eased the tension. Don't just learn to play or preach; do it skilfully. Of course, you were born for it, but what will take you to the top is your ability to translate your talents.

There are no shortcuts in life. The world will overlook and belittle you at some point. But you should keep learning how to communicate your gifts ahead of the greatest opportunity of your life.

In the next chapter, we will look at how a sustained opportunity can create sustained blessings. If you hold onto what you are doing consistently, it will yield the future you desire.

OPPORTUNITY

A sustained opportunity is a sustained blessing.

An opportunity is an advantageous and strategic chance. It is our most favourable, auspicious and promising condition in life. It is a set time that makes it possible to achieve one's goals. It is also described as a lucky chance, good time or great occasion. It provides us with a life-changing experience. Sometimes an opportunity may seem like hard work. It could be unfavourable at times. But every sustained opportunity can be turned into a blessing.

Opportunities are never lost; people simply

take them. What you consider a rejection could be a leverage for education. Opportunity is the way in which God recruits the willing talent. Failure is not the end but an opportunity to re-strategise and work on your goals again. Where some people see defeat, others see a chance to fight again. To identify an opportunity in any area of life, you need diligence and perseverance. After all, opportunities do not fall out of the thin air. What most people think is a disadvantage could be your greatest opportunity to manifest the glory of God. In every adversity, there is a seed of advantage. Every endeavour is an opportunity to manifest your talent and purpose on earth. Never underestimate your apprenticeship; it is not only the early stage of your career but also an opportunity to move to the top.

Anytime you sustain an opportunity, you have access to a blessing, a breakthrough or a victory. Though some people are gifted, they cannot prove their worth because they cannot handle opportunities.

In addition to being the killer of a giant, David was also a "cunning player on a harp" (1 Samuel 16:16). God had anointed him to be a king. A person with that kind of destiny should have been given the opportunity to sit with governors and lawmakers but instead, he was to entertain the troubled king. 1 Samuel 16:23 says *"And it came to pass, when the evil spirit from God was upon Saul, that David took an harp, and played with his hand: so Saul was refreshed, and was well, and the evil spirit departed from him."* Someone else would have frowned and walked away from that opportunity, but not David. Your present venture may not look like a great opening, but it becomes a blessing when you sustain and nourish it.

What you are doing now could be a clue to your greatness in life. And your ability to nourish it will determine your height. Gold and diamonds are hidden in the roughest places on earth. The opportunity that will set you for greatness may be entrenched in a challenge but as you sustain the opportunity, you activate a blessing. Absalom and Solomon had the same father. One was a fool while the other was the wisest man that ever lived on earth. You cannot change your life until you change whose voice you honour. Let God speak to you about your current situation. It might seem inconsequential but beyond the surface, it is an avenue for greatness.

How Do You Sustain an Opportunity?

1. Have Hope! It Does Not Disappoint.

Hope is a feeling that something desirable is likely to happen. It is the state of having high expectations even when an anticipated event looks bleak. When it seems you have been forgotten, hope does not disappoint. Hope sustained David. It was hope that led him to the battlefield after his heroic act of killing a lion and a bear. He knew he carried something. Hope sustains an opportunity. At times, I walk down to the bus station with a heavy heart, but what keeps me going is the hope that it will come to an end someday.

2. Have Faith in the Promise.

Faith sustains your confidence in God's promises. And it will help you to overcome the most humiliating experience in life. Sometimes when we hear people's testimonies, we are in awe of the tremendous miracle they experienced. But what induced the miracle was faith in God's promise. No matter how far it looks, never take your eyes or faith off the promise.

Faith in the promise can preserve an opportunity into a great blessing. David told Saul, "...Let no man's heart fail because of him; thy servant will go and fight with this Philistine" (1 Samuel 17:32). David's arrival at the palace was an opportunity, but it took faith to face Goliath. When you have faith in the promise, you automatically turn your situation around for good.

3. Stay Confident.

Job 19:25 says, "For I know that my redeemer liveth, and that he shall stand at the latter day upon the earth." To sustain an opportunity in life, you must maintain a positive and confident attitude. A lack of confidence in God and in your ability can impair opportunities. The worst disability is a bad attitude towards life. To turn your opportunities into great prospects, stay confident in your lowest ebb. To sustain an opportunity, you need to stay on the confidence ladder. Once your confidence leaves, the opportunity may be gone. Every setback aims to either make you concede defeat or to make you a better person. When the tide of life blows and the vicissitudes of life set in, don't surrender what you believe in because your belief is the key to unlocking the future.

4. Give a New Meaning to the Problem.

Do not allow the challenges of life define you. If you can be defined, you can be confined. Although setbacks are capable of helping you, they fail to help when you allow them to define you. Stop looking at where you are; look at what you can be. Don't spend time brooding over sorrows and mistakes of the past. For every setback, there is a recovery or a comeback. Genesis 50:20 (AMP) says, *"As for you, you thought evil against me, but God meant it for good, to bring about that many people should be kept alive, as they are this day."* Every occurrence is meant for your good! And for every opportunity, there will be a momentary tragedy. Learn to give your problems a new meaning. What kept Joseph going in the pit, prison and the podium was his determination to give every problem a new meaning.

5. Be Faithful in Every Endeavour.

According to Luke 16:10-12, *"He that is faithful in that which is least is faithful also in much: and he that is unjust in the least is unjust also in much. If therefore ye have not been faithful in the unrighteous mammon, who will commit to your trust the true riches? And if ye have not been faithful in that which is another man's, who shall give you that which is your own."*

The synonyms of faithfulness include honesty, truthfulness, integrity, reliability and dependability. When you are faithful as an amateur, you easily sustain it as a professional. Many potentials have disappeared into obscurity because they toyed with unfaithfulness. Can you be trusted? Can you be entrusted with a responsibility? No undertaking is too small to be an opportunity for a blessing. You must always discharge your duties with faithfulness and honesty. You may not have supervisors when you are in isolation, but you must remain faithful.

Faithfulness has three major levels. Faithfulness in that which is least, in monetary matters and in what belongs to another person. In Isolation, the key to unlocking your future is faithfulness in these three levels. Before you are set over a hundred people, God will first set you over ten. If you are diligent, hardworking and committed over ten, then you can be set over a hundred. I often tell people that if they cannot pay a tithe of a hundred pounds out of a thousand-pound check, they should not expect God to set them over tens of thousands. If you have not been faithful with the "unrighteous mammon, who will commit to your trust the true riches?" In the same regard, if you are set over 'least', you must be faithful.

Some subordinates discharge their duties with indignation because they feel they are being undervalued or disrespected. But a sustained opportunity can become a major breakthrough. Before God gives us a great venture, He would first us on a small one while in isolation. Faithfulness in the little things of life is the pathway to gaining the strength you need to move to the top.

6. Understand the Law of Respect.

To sustain an opportunity in life, never devalue the honour of service. Opportunities come to us in disguise. And the law of respect states that you attract what you respect in life. The current younger generation does not seem to put any premium on values, culture and history. Never lose respect for an assigned responsibility. Some people have lost great opportunities because they lost respect for their duties. There is a correlation between success and respect. The anointing you respect is the anointing you attract. When you are in isolation, never lose sight of the main thing in life because you attract what you value.

7. Maintain the Law of Repetition.

To sustain an opportunity, you must maintain a daily routine. We are as good as our daily routine. A routine is a sequence of actions, instructions, procedure and custom regularly followed for performing a task. Our daily routines fuel and sustain our opportunities in life. What you constantly do, follow, hear and practise will eventually bear fruits. In my days as an apprentice in church, I practised punctuality and smart dressing. I never cut corners in my assignments. Repetition creates a routine, and routines create habits. Successful people have great habits. In isolation David mastered the sling shot that killed Goliath. Joseph was an interpreter of dreams way before he arrived at the palace. Jesus had a custom of going to the synagogue to read the scroll. *"And he came to Nazareth, where he had been brought up: and, as his custom was, he went into the synagogue on the sabbath day, and stood up to read."* — Luke 4:16

Note the following points about the law of routine:

- The law of routine creates resilience and strength in you.
- The law of routine can get you whatever you want in life.
- Operating the law of routine defiles resistance, opposition and hostility.
- The law of routine eliminates distractions and anxieties.
- The law of routine overrules discouragement and dismay.
- The law of routine removes doubts and creates expectations.

Your routine can turn your weakness into a strength. In life, your priorities show what you value. And consistency sustains assignments and creates success. A loss, for instance, creates a desire in us for change. And hunger is not a bad thing because it shows you are dissatisfied.

8. Be Determined in Every Endeavour.

To sustain opportunities, you must cultivate the fortitude to move ahead and settle issues conclusively in your mind. Where there is determination, resilience and steadfastness, there is a way. In all your endeavours, you must be determined. It gives you the power to overcome obstacles. It should not surprise you that the greatest oak was once a little nut that held its ground. Determination will not only sustain an opportunity but it will also activate a blessing. Your decision to throw in the towel could be a calculated strategy from hell to make you leave the place of blessing.

Albert Einstein said, "It's not that I'm so smart, it's just that I stay with problems longer." The key to being at the top and staying there is doggedness. Every time you sustain a given opportunity, you get a blessing. You may be a cleaner in a hotel, an attendant in an airport, a cook in a primary school or a teaching assistant in a low-grade school. Keep at it. To succeed in life, you need to find something to hold on to and something to motivate and inspire you.

9. Every Opportunity is Tied to a Promise.

Opportunities are tied to a promise or a breakthrough; they are a stepping stone to greatness. The greatest opportunities in life are often disguised. We tend to see the obstacles instead of the blessings to come. If you ask successful people, they will tell you how they once held on to a venture that didn't look promising. But the lessons they garnered were worth it in the end. When you realise that what you are doing is tied to a promise, it raises your expectations. It activates your hope and strength. There is nothing like wasted time. What is wasted is an opportunity. Live life with the view that something good will come out of it.

Apostle Paul admonished us in Philippians 2:14 (AMP) to *"Do all things without grumbling and fault finding and complaining [against God] and questioning and doubting [among yourselves]."*

Regardless of where you are at the moment, my friend, don't do things with grumbling and fault finding. It kills purpose and deflects hope. Set your eyes on the promise, and work with your heart.

10. Every Opportunity Leads to a Purpose.

Every opportunity leads to a greater cause in life. God's purposes are often tied to openings. Every greatness was once entrenched in an opportunity. Whatever you are asked to do in life, either accidentally or intentionally, has a godly purpose. In God, there is no accident or mistakes. Nothing is a mishap with God. When we don't know the purpose of a thing, abuse is inevitable. It would have been difficult to explain to Moses that looking after some cattle would give him a degree in emancipation strategy. It would not have made sense to tell Joseph that his imprisonment was an internship for a palace assignment. If David had been told that his hardship was the special training that would aid the fulfilment of his destiny, he would have dismissed it. Sometimes it doesn't have to make sense to you. God's ways often seem foolish to the undiscerning. It did not make sense that to save humanity, God had to sacrifice His beloved son. But God knows better. Life is also intertwined with opportunities which are often disguised as hard work and senseless endeavours.

11. Every Opportunity Comes With Rejection.

Opportunities come with a certain amount of rejection. The greater the opportunity, the greater the rejection. Rejection is a negative response; it means to be disowned and snubbed as you discharge your duty. Joseph's brothers hated him not because of his coat of many colours but because he was the father's favourite. He was the errand boy for the old man. Perhaps he sat with his father all day, learning from him. Though he was rejected, he was accepted by his enemies in the end. Many people jump at an opportunity without thinking of the responsibility and rejection that accompany it. Rejection is to the degree you accept it. And it measures your determination and willpower in life.

12. Opportunities Open Doors.

A sustained opportunity can open doors for you. When in isolation, you will find yourself doing some things that you do not enjoy. But you must remember that a sustained opportunity activates a divine door. A door is a break, opening or a chance, especially one that offers some kind of advantage. It is also a superior position you have over others. Doors give access. There are four doors associated with opportunities:

a. Physical Doors

These doors open and close at will. They open when we apply force. The amount of force you apply to a physical door determines how wide it opens to you. These doors require you to pull them open with some amount of determination and willpower.

As written in Matthew 11:12, *"And from the days of John the Baptist until now the kingdom of heaven suffereth violence, and the violent take it by force."* Just as the kingdom of God requires some amount of violence, you may need to be violent to open physical doors. How you open a physical door depends on how far you want to go. How much do you want it? If you want to enter a building so badly, you will stay there until the door opens.

b. Doors With Codes

These doors open and close when you activate the right codes. Such doors are seen in secure buildings around the world. You don't need strength to pull it open. As long as you have the code, the door will open.

> *"And looking up to heaven, he sighed, and saith unto him, Ephphatha, that is, Be opened. And straightway his ears were opened, and the string of his tongue was loosed, and he spake plain."* **Mark 7:34-35**

Here was a blind man who also had a speech impediment. This man had everything that should make him hear and see, but the codes were corrupted. Jesus simply activated his sight and hearing by punching the right codes, and the doors opened immediately. Serving under a boss is one of the right codes you need to unlock your potential. These kinds of doors require revelation, supernatural intervention and divine inspiration. It is the kind of knowledge and technical know-how that is beyond human competence.

c. Doors of Presence

These are automatic doors. They will only open when you are in close proximity. Such doors don't respond to codes or physical force but proximity, closeness and connection. Doctors don't receive training from mechanics nor do lawyers train carpenters because each profession is unique and requires the right tutor. Similarly, your opportunities in life are tied to a unique door. An opportunity that requires the door of presence will not open to any other kind of door. Why did Pharaoh's daughter take Moses to the palace? Why did she have to bathe in that particular river that day? She was the door of presence that God needed to activate the opportunity to rescue the children of Israel. Always remember that your location determines your elevation.

d. Doors of Timing

The door of timing has time constraints. If you miss the opening, you have to start all over. Many people stepped out of line because the world underestimated them, but they have evaporated from the scene. Your life is tied to an opportunity, and every opportunity is tied to a door that opens according to its time. These kinds of doors are connected to times and seasons. You can't force it open; you can't use codes or associations. You must wait for the correct timing.

The Tragedy of a Wasted Opportunity

Under this subheading, we will examine the reactions of some men and women in the Bible when they had access to certain opportunities.

1. The Complexity of Gehazi's Opportunity (2 Kings 5:15-27)

When people live carelessly because of fine things, they lose their significance. Gehazi was so close to the anointing, but he got distracted. He had a great opportunity but lacked the understanding of the opportunity. Let's assume he had been with prophet Elisha for a little over a decade. He could possibly be living in poverty. Elisha's refusal to take Naaman's offerings pushed him over the edge. All these years, he dreamt of prestige and status. Gehazi's problem was that while God told Elisha not to take those gifts, God never told him anything. That was his dilemma. Why shouldn't he take anything from Naaman? Some anointing and calling require a certain lifestyle. Gehazi was supposed to inherit the anointing on Elisha, but he misunderstood why he was in the presence of the man of God.

Many promising talents are wasted because their owners had a hard time understanding why they could not do certain things? Why can't they go out partying like everybody else? Why couldn't Gehazi take the offerings from the foreign general? When God gave the instructions to prophet Elijah, he wasn't included. So why did it affect him? He had a family to feed, probably a life to live and a future to take care of.

Gehazi's Quagmires:
- Gehazi served in one of the greatest heights of ministry and was a candidate for the anointing.
- All along, he carried an invisible wound while he was in contact with an opportunity.
- Gehazi was never mentioned as a great servant; the emphasis was on the fact that he became a leper for life.
- He might have disrespected or undervalued the opportunity given to him.
- Perhaps he was never ready for the opportunity, and this led to his tragic end.

2. The Lean Opportunities o-f Joseph

While in the dungeon, Joseph had a slim chance of fulfilling his dream as a rescuer of his people. He had eleven abled brothers, but God picked him. Isn't it amazing when God picks a flawed material and crafts gold out of it? He was sold as a slave. He spent many years in jail, serving a crime he never committed. He was denied the opportunity of brotherhood. His chances of reaching the top were lean. Yet he sustained the opportunity, and it turned out to be a blessing. Joseph could have folded his arms or sat in despair and let the lean opportunity slip by. Although he was in isolation, he worked as much as any man in the palace. His brothers didn't believe him. Potiphar didn't believe him, and Potiphar's wife fabricated lies to get him into jail.

In the jailhouse, he went on different errands and on such errands, he came across a destiny helper who turned his life of pain into gain. Never complain on a bad day. Don't kill yourself for making a detour from some strict family values. Before we access opportunities, we will first be dumped in isolation. To get to the top, you must pass through isolation. Joseph was to be one of the greatest economists and prime minister of his time. But he had to spend some time in prison, serving tables, mopping the floor, and serving a sentence for a crime he never committed. Genesis 50:20 (MSG) reveals how Joseph viewed his prison experience. Despite the long years of pain and denial, he focused on the brighter side. And he said, *"As far as I am concerned, God turned into good what you meant for evil. He brought me to the high position I have today so I could save the lives of many people."*

Did Joseph know this the first day he stepped into prison? No! But he maximised the lean opportunity and eventually arrived at the top. How many young men and women have flipped into oblivion because they felt the opportunity was not big enough? 1 Corinthians 4:2 tells us that *"Moreover, it is required in stewards, that a man be found faithful."* How many times have we said it's just a small church, just a few people or just some bunch of old folks? Although no one is watching, we must be found faithful. No matter how small or insignificant it might be, never cut corners.

Joseph's Opportunities

- All odds were stacked against him and his talent, hence he had a slim chance of success.
- He could have used his time in jail to be bitter and complain about his brothers' actions.
- He lost everything, but he sustained the opportunity he had.
- He never lost the respect for repetition, and he respected the opportunity to serve.
- Though gifted, he was humiliated. However, he never discarded his opportunity.
- When an opportunity is sustained, it becomes maximised.

3. Gideon's Disguised Opportunity

God often uses our greatest need to prepare us for our calling in life. Gideon's need was a concealed opportunity to bring him to a place of reliance on God. Sometimes, a tragic childhood or a poor upbringing is an avenue to build one's resilience for what is to come. Many of the world's richest people do not have rich parents. Some of them never had the luxury of a beautiful upbringing. But God sometimes uses fright to teach us how to fight because where there is no pain, there is no gain.

Gideon was a young man with a bright future, yet his life was covered in poverty and complexities. He believed that his forefathers were redeemed from Egypt by the mighty hand of God, but he found himself in a complex web of delay, defeat and regret. The angel of the Lord found him in a winepress.

> *"And there came an angel of the LORD, and sat under an oak which was in Ophrah, that pertained unto Joash the Abi-ezrite: and his son Gideon threshed wheat by the winepress, to hide it from the Midianites."* **Judges 6:11**

When everybody else was gone, he went to the winepress right in the midst of terrorist attacks and intimidation. Many of the soldiers hid in dens and caves. However, this poor young man stayed in the winepress. During that time, a winepress was a factory where wine was produced by squeezing the juice out of grapes. It was hard work. When other strong young men in the city could have joined Gideon, they went into hiding. Gideon's opportunity was disguised in hard work.

What Were His Opportunities?
- Gideon had always thought God had deserted him.
- He lived each day with dread, disappointment and frustration.
- He didn't know his predicament was an opportunity in disguise.
- He was a mighty man of valour yet under a spell of despair and hopelessness.
- All along, it was an opportunity waiting to happen.
- What he thought was an expression of disbelief was the key to his calling.

4. The Camel's Test for Rebekah

The book of Genesis 24:1-7 reveals a business principle called the camel's test. Abraham had sent his servant, Eliezer, to his hometown to look for a wife for Isaac. When Eliezer got to a well in the town, he prayed that the damsel that would offer his ten camels and him water would be Isaac's wife. The young lady, Rebekah, had no idea that a man would trigger an opportunity for her to activate God's plan for mankind. But when Eliezer threw the challenge to Rebekah, she obliged. She fetched drinking water for him and the camels. Many have missed the opportunity to be part of something big because it looked small at first. The Bible says Eliezer *"...stood gazing at her in silence, waiting to know if the Lord had made his trip prosperous."* (Genesis 24:21)

What if Rebekah had said she was busy and running late? What if she could not bring herself to fetch water for a stranger and his camels? Perhaps she had been praying for a husband. Without a doubt, she had some goals, but she got a test, and she passed. Every test in life is a testimony in the making. She sustained the available opportunity by providing water for Eliezer and his camels to drink. Eliezer's choice of test could have been informed by the fact that Abraham, being a prosperous man, had a habit of entertaining strangers (Genesis 18:1). As such, Rebekah must pass the camel's test before she could join the family. Rebekah was in isolation, but what took her to the top was an opportunity.

The camel's test:
- The camel's test comes unawares and in the most unlikely places.
- Opportunity comes in strange places.
- Whenever you sustain your opportunity, you activate an atmosphere.
- Running errands is never a disadvantage.
- Every testimony is preceded by a test.
- What if Rebekah failed to recognise that some awkward situations could be a platform for greatness?
- Sometimes, in the land of opportunities, the test comes before the lesson.

1. The Dangerous Manoeuvre of Esther's Opportunity

At times, opportunities come with dangerous manoeuvres. Although Esther had become a queen, she faced the threat of being executed. Life is full of twists and turns that require us to be circumspect. Esther's story is that of a sustained opportunity. She was from a minority background contesting for a beauty pageant in a foreign land. The likelihood of failure was great, but she sustained her opportunity, and it turned out to be a blessing.

After she became the queen, one of the king's aides, Haman, devised a plot to eliminate all the Jews. His plan to destroy the Jews became an important opportunity for Esther to intervene for her people. Recall that before the contest, she never disclosed who she was. Though she had become the queen, she neither forgot her roots nor the kindness of her uncle, Mordecai. Esther was not like those who'd forget their background once they're in a land of opportunity. There are people in my life I cannot do without. When I was a poor church boy, some people helped me to become what I am today. How can I ever forget them? As the day of execution drew near, and Esther was brought in the know, she made a move to help her people.

The dynamics of opportunity can be seen in her selflessness. It also shows that every opportunity comes with an assignment. Esther never excluded herself from the struggle; doing that would have been an abuse of opportunity. In life, opportunities often surface in unlikely places. And they sometimes require a dangerous manoeuvre. Esther was willing to go against the law. Despite being a queen, she could not go before the king uninvited. And it would be disastrous if for some reason the king disapproved of her appearance. But she was ready to take the risk. If all went as planned, the king would extend the golden sceptre to her, and she would find favour in his sight. It was a daring task, but she resolved to do it regardless.

Every opportunity has some amount of risks. It is better to take a risk than to make a bunch of excuses for doing nothing. Esther was resolute in her decision. In Esther 4:16, she said, "If I perish, I perish!" These words kept her going. Never allow excuses to come between you and your golden opportunity because your biggest chance to reach the top is how well you manage opportunities.

Esther's opportunities:
- Every opportunity given to you has some amount of risks.
- Your greatest opportunity may surface in

unlikely places on earth.
- Every opportunity has a dangerous manoeuvre.
- How you manage opportunities determines how you move to the top.
- Every opportunity has an assignment attached to it.

LEADERSHIP

Great leaders are often made in a place of isolation.

Leaders need to die to self. In isolation, we are broken, we have no rights, and we are sold out to a purpose and God. Until that happens, there will still be too much of self and the old mindset. Before God makes you a leader, He will need a system to work on your weakness and groom you on your assignment. Some temperaments and experiences may inhibit you from responding to the call of God. The place of isolation thus becomes a surgical hub to remove these traits. Some experiences that you consider weapons of greatness may also need to be refined and enhanced.

In every human head, there is a mind. Within every mind is a belief system. Within every belief system is a shaper. And within every shaper is an agenda. For most of us, by the time we achieve greatness, our belief system is marred by the shaper. Some people crumble because of their belief system and the shaper. However, isolation, overhauls the belief system and redefines the shaper. Every shaper has an agenda. For Adolf Hitler, the shaper was sinister, and the plan was diabolical. For Winston Churchill, the shaper was determination and resilience; the agenda was no retreat and no surrender.

Many leaders will probably tell you they had to cultivate a belief system when they were in a state of oblivion. What you are is God's gift to you. What you make out of yourself is your gift to God.

Belief Systems

Belief systems are the stories we tell ourselves to define our sense of reality. This could be in the form of religion, political affiliation, philosophy, or spirituality among many other things. We are controlled by our beliefs, which are influenced by different factors. Our knowledge of a specific topic, how we were raised, where we grew up, and even peer pressure create and change our belief systems. Life is such a big classroom. Every day we are being taught by nature and adversities. And these changing scenarios shape our beliefs.

In this section, you will see how God crafts leadership out of you by interfering with your belief systems. Great leaders develop through a never-ending process of self-study, education, training and experience. God often remodels their belief system when they are isolated. Your exclusion is never an accident. It is a pathway to greatness. My managerial and leadership skills are not from the books I read; they stem from the times of loneliness in the backside of the wilderness. During that time, my belief system was revised. I learnt that leadership had nothing to do with lording over others but by being selfless. Today, it feels as though leaders are celebrities and superstars.

The shaper is how we have been packaged in life. The environment you grew up in determines the height you can aspire to in life. The kind of school you were enrolled in speaks volumes about your excellence, too. In sociology, it is said that we are products of our environment. An abusive father will raise an abusive husband. A promiscuous mother will raise a licentious wife. Although every rule has exceptions, what we are or will become is mostly a result of the shaper.

What is a Shaper?

A shaper is all that contributes to who you are — your temperament, persona, disposition and personality. It also has to do with your background and experiences. Your shaper include your place of birth, how you were raised, and the people you interacted with. Some of us from Africa have a sinister shaper — poverty, low self-esteem and poor perception of ourselves. Most Europeans are raised with a little "silver spoon in their mouth". Here's what I mean by that. I once taught in a high school in the UK. These fantastic top-set year-ten boys had no idea about their privileges. It was obvious in their attitude towards lessons, information, and learning materials.

So, one day, I returned to my motherland and took a video of my old high school. Some of them were shocked. They wondered how I knew so much in such an environment. The classroom had no lights, no carpets; the table and chairs were dilapidated, and the classrooms looked odd compared with what they had. To be honest, things are changing in Africa, but many students still struggle to access education. By comparing the same year group from Africa with European students, you realise the shaper had a severe impact on their confidence, attitude and aptitude. We are what we are because of the shaper. If you are from the ghetto, the shaper would have modelled you to ghetto standards. If you are taken into a more developed society, you will struggle because the shaper has made you unfit.

As soon as I became a born-again Christian, I had a new shaper. Although born in extreme poverty, there was a shaper in me that overhauled how I perceived myself. I saw the future from a different perspective. Even though I knew little about how I would turn out eventually, I had an inkling I was going to be a teacher, minister, or speaker. What can you do to repair what the shaper has impaired? How would you be a better wife if you had not read a book on marriage? What do you think you will do, if you were given a leadership position when you have not read a book on leadership?

Throughout the scriptures, God isolated people to work on the shaper that has messed them up. I may not be a well-known preacher, but I have decided not to allow the shaper in my past to wreck my future. Now that nobody knows who I am, I am ready to let the Holy Spirit, my new shaper, revamp what used to be to what it is supposed to be.

> *And I will ask the Father, and He will give you another Comforter (Counsellor, Helper, Intercessor, Advocate, Strengthener, and Standby), that He may remain with you forever.* **John 14:16**

This is it! Perhaps you are at a forever juncture in at the moment. I pray that God will give you another comforter — shaper of your future. How Bill Gates, Tiger Woods and David Beckham arrived at the top is the job of the shaper in their minds. How they fare at the top is the agenda. What motivated Adolf Hitler? What made Sir Alex Ferguson win trophies for Manchester United? What made Arsene Wenger sit on the same seat for the gunners for almost twenty years? There is a belief system in their mind. And in that system, there is a shaper with an agenda.

What is Your Agenda in Life?

A universal rule says, "everybody is born with an agenda." How the agenda is carried out, however, is determined by the shaper. In life, you are either remembered or dismembered by society. As much as you are willing to be at the top, work on your shaper, and the agenda will fall into place. For a young man desiring to get married, this is the agenda: a young woman dreaming of a big family. What will make the dream a reality is how you handle your shaper. And how you fare will be determined by many factors.

I know I was not the best student in my class nor the best at football even though I love the game. I am not the best preacher or pastor in my generation. Yet, it was "written in the stars" that I may end up leading something – the agenda. What will add quality to the future is the shaper. Work on the shaper, and the agenda will live out itself.

In every isolation phase, God teaches us to be great leaders. Sometimes we may not look glamorous in the making. You may be unconvincing, but God has a way of bringing the best out of flawed materials. In moving to the top, accountability is leadership. Leadership is accountability; accountability is responsibility. And responsibility is responding to divine ability. Many aspiring leaders of the 21st century lack accountability. Some lobbied for greatness but cannot be responsible to anybody or for anything. Yet they occupy the loftiest positions. Unfortunately, leadership doesn't have a one-size-fits-all definition.

We all have different ideas about what it means to be a good leader. When I was an aspiring pastor, I had an idea about leadership. I saw it as being the boss, the top guy, and the mafia-style of exerting authority. But in the backside of the desert, I learnt a lot that one must be selfless in order to make an impact. The higher you go, the lower you should be in heart and spirit. The wrong you see in your environment is what you are called to correct. If you were raised under an ineffective leader, your assignment is to fix what they could not do. We must never repeat and perpetuate the atrocities of our predecessors.

In isolation, the primary objective is to learn how to be accountable. We will soon examine the story of the talent in the Bible. But can you imagine people who have not been faithful in a five-people business or loyal to a ten-people church? In the story of the talent, a master was travelling to a remote country, so he called his servants and entrusted them with talents (the original translation says his goods). He placed in their hands responsibility which is tantamount to leadership.

> *For it is like a man who was about to take a long journey, and he called his servants together and entrusted them with his property.* **Matthew 25:14 AMP**

The story reads like it was a great house with lots of servants, yet he chose these three people to manage years of priced assets, enviable riches, and perhaps life savings. In the story, each servant was given the talent according his ability. The saddest thing about life is that sometimes I meet people serving as subordinates who don't know what they're doing. It is a tragedy to waste an opportunity. Even if you are not given something to do, there is always something you can do. Do it with skill and proficiency.

The Five-Talent Group

"To one he gave five talents [probably about $5,000], to another two, to another one--to each in proportion to his ability. Then he departed and left the country"
Matthew 25:15

Many gifted people become irrelevant suddenly. They had five talents but were never responsible for what they had. They were moving in a cycle of poverty and did not make it big not because they weren't good, but because they forgot that leadership is accountability, accountability is a responsibility, and responsibility is responding to divine ability. Despite their tremendous abilities, they are at the bottom of the spectrum. You can have five talents, but if you only put in effort for one talent, it will eventually be usurped from you. This is the reason a brilliant child suddenly goes out of relevance because he was not accountable for the gift given.

There is an element of divinity where God opens a portal for you, and tap-tap-bam you land in the limelight of fame. It looks great, right? What if you are called to give a five-minute exhortation at your sister's birthday? What if it is the portal

God will use for your greatness? What if you mess it up because you never took time to polish your talking skills?

The five talents in our society today have turned to drugs; they have become addicts because they are not accountable. The reason you are not at the top is not because you aren't good or you aren't given a fair chance. It's because the great man on His journey has given you five talents. And you must be found faithful in all (1 Corinthians 4:2). No one admires gold in its raw state but with a little effort, it has a DNA that turns servants to royals, ordinary into extraordinary and poverty into prominence.

The Two-Talent People

"... to another two ... to each in proportion to his own ability" **Matthew 25:15b**

These people know they don't have much, but they can move forward with little effort. But they often fall off into apathy and lethargy. A great man of God once said, "Favour isn't fair". Sometimes you would see somebody with two talent doing a five-talent job because they were accountable and responsible. This category sometimes give up on themselves; when they look at the five-talent man, they become despondent. Many two-talent people are stuck in a rut of despair on the road to the top.

You may have a two-talent gift, but genuine efforts can land you in the limelight. I am one of these boys who may not be overly clever as a child, but I knew I could do it once I applied myself to something. This is the classic example of a two-talent person. You may think you are an average person, but if you apply yourself to something you stand a chance of making it big. When you become a leader, what will be your legacy? That day is coming but now that you are a little village,, cultivate leadership skills.

Do you know the thousands of gifted people wasted in the land of by and by? They could be two-talent people who must be accountable and responsible for their divine ability. A five-talent effort can break the status quo in your life. The greater the anointing, the greater the movement of the spirit.

One-Talent people

"...to another one--to each in proportion to his own personal ability." **Matthew 25:15**

The one-talent person with five talented efforts will arrive at the top. A popular statement says, "The majority carries the vote." The fact that you are a one-talent man or woman does not make you a minority. Many five-talent people will fail, and many one-talent people will continue to rule the world. This may shock you. But in the parable, the one-talent man seemed to have been treated harshly because Jesus expected more from him.

Many people with one talent are ruling our world today. What can Sir Alex Ferguson of Manchester United do apart from what he has become? What could Tiger Woods have done apart from golf? What could T D Jakes have done in life apart from what he is doing? What exactly could Oprah Winfrey be if not a talk show host? Winfrey may not be able to sing or draw, but just sit in a paddy seat and talk. Today she is a multi-millionaire. She could have murmured and complained that the only gift she had is to sit and talk, but she didn't.

Even if you are disadvantaged, you cannot bury what you have. Never discount your talent because it is the blueprint to greatness. Oprah got her big break and landed a job in a radio station while still in high school and began co-anchoring the local evening news at the age of 19. She may have been on the bus going home every night grumbling about friends who can sing, dance and perhaps are extremely talented at something she is not good at. In life, if you think you are a one-talent man or woman, you are a candidate for greatness.

We are the kind of people who think we don't have enough education like 'Robert' or 'Roberta'. My father could not read or write, but I only got to know it in my teens. He demanded to see my school report every term. He would visit my school to have a long chat with my teacher. He had a friend who could only communicate in English language. Then, if you have never been to school before, you are not entitled to communicate in English, but my father did. He might have only one talent, but he was accountable. He was a rich man in his own right, with coaches and workers under him in the transport business. He was above his peers who could read and write. He was a one-talent man with lots of five-talent effort.

It is a Tragedy of Life

The irony is that five-talent men or women who put in the one-talent effort will get results. A five-talent man or woman who only puts in a two-talent effort will get some results. Even if they put in a one-talent effort, they will get a result. On one talent, a man will reap with a one-talent-effort mentality. Most of the world's richest people may not have gone to Harvard, Oxford or Cambridge. Yet they are at the top of the food-chain ladder. Education is good to have, but lack of education m shouldn't stop you from getting to the top.

What can you do from your 'here and now' before that opportunity comes calling? In every isolation, you are cultivating leadership. Leadership is accountability. And there is only one route to the top. If you cannot be trusted with the simple responsibilities, how then can you be trusted with higher tasks? Wherever you are today corresponds to the effort you have invested in your talent. A one-talent man with a five-talent mindset will outlast a five-talent man with a one-talent mindset. This is the tragedy of life. So, never complain that you are not gifted or talented. When babies are born, they clench their fists. We held our job description and talents on arrival; don't lose yours.

God uses some leadership models to teach us during the seasons of isolation. God does not raise his generals without teaching them accountability. Whatever state you are today is a clue to what you will become tomorrow. In isolation, responsibility is a prerequisite for promotion. And one of the main courses on the menu will be how to wear accountability, how to operate with responsibility, and how you respond to divine ability.

Isolation: Davidic Model

The Davidic model takes insignificance and turns it into a great accomplishment.

God wanted to replace King Saul with a successor who would be a man after his own heart. When Saul reigned, God had a replacement in isolation. I believe there is a whole new generation in isolation. They are tending sheep and running errands at the backside of the desert and some of us may have given up on them. Yet at the appointed time, these men and women will emerge in the palace. David's job was to tend the sheep. If this boy walked past you on a pathway, you may not recognise him as a lion and bear killer. There were no signs that he was a giant killer walking around. He was one of the greatest kings in history. In contrast, he was described as a naughty and proud chap, who had come in to squint at the battle.

> *And Eliab his eldest brother heard when he spake unto the men; and Eliab's anger was kindled against David, and he said, why camest thou down hither? and with whom hast thou left those few sheep in the wilderness? I know thy pride, and the naughtiness of thine heart; for thou art come down that thou mightest see the battle.* **1 Samuel 17:28**

God uses the Davidic model to raise the least likely to be the most likely in life. Sometimes, the least of us could be the greatest among us. Here was a lad at the backside of the wilderness, unknown, untrained, and isolated from all luxury. We are still not sure of his age, but surely in his teens. He arrived at a scene destined to make him move from limitation to a manifestation. This is the kind of portal God opens on our behalf after we finished from the school of isolation. Then, opportunity meets timing. How prepared are you? David was an errand boy for the family, probably the one they thought could not amount to anything in life. Yet he had developed his skills.

> *Among all these soldiers there were seven hundred chosen men who were left-handed, each of whom could sling a stone at a hair and not miss.* **Judges 20:16 NIV**

In the time they lived in, a slingshot was not a hobby tool but an office in the army by left-handed men who were trained to shoot at the width of human air and not to miss. It looks like a one-talent thing. Not glamorous or fashionable. However, with a five-talent effort, an army general was born. David was not trained by the military. He knew he had a sling and sheep, but what could the future be? He trained himself. What is exciting about slinging a shot at trees, stray sheep and wayward goats? Whatever gets repeated gets rewarded.

Remember, one talent is no excuse. Just keep practising, keep being consistent, and keep reporting to work on time every day. If it's a church or a pantry, be diligent. A portal will open one day. What if he had arrived on the battlefield without the slingshot? What if he thought he would be teased for carrying a slingshot? David was a songwriter, a psalmist and a warrior. He was a worshipper and a shepherd, too. Whenever he played his musical instrument, evil spirits were driven out of kings. But what took him to the top was the slingshot. One-talent man or woman with a five-talent effort will make it to the top. Before David's rise to stardom, he was a shepherd boy. He went to the battlefield to give lunch to his brothers. He was ostracised by family. When the prophet showed up, his parents and brothers never called for him. He was not relevant. It was just by chance. But the boldness of this young man was impeccable. He knew he couldn't miss if he was given the opportunity to use his sling. Again, leadership is accountability, accountability is responsibility and responsibility is responding to divine ability. This model is perfect for a one-talent man or woman. You must be accountable for what you have been given. Time and chance will happen to us all. David arrived at the right time when his journey to greatness was right before him.

Isolation: Mosaic Model

Moses' parents had two siblings before him — Miriam and Aaron. Did you know Moses was not named by his parents? Jochebed and Amram couldn't name the boy because he glowed in the dark. The Bible described him as a goodly child (Exodus 2:3).

Miriam represents the five-talent. She was a heck of a musician. She had it all together. She could sing. She was also a brilliant and outstanding leader. Out of the shadows, she stepped forth innocently and appeared to be curious at the screaming baby and puzzled princess, asking if she would like her to get a Hebrew nurse. Miriam kept her silence and did not reveal her relation to the baby and the nurse she secured. Thus, the ready wit of Miriam, a girl of ten to twelve years old, saved her brother whom the Princess called Moses. When he became the deliverer, Miriam must have been grateful for her share in preserving her baby brother from the cruel fate of other Hebrew infants.

If she was about 12 years of age when Moses was born, and he spent 40 years in Egypt, then another 40 in the land of Midian before the dramatic episode of the Red Sea, Miriam was about 92 years old before the deliverance of Israel. Miriam was a five-talent person. Till today, her songs, poems and her style of praise and worship are still exemplified in the world of powerful praise and worship. Aaron, on the other hand, was a two-talent person. He was born in Egypt three years before Moses. God made him Moses' mouthpiece because he was a gifted speaker. This amazing family was chosen by God to advance the deliverance of the Israelites.

In the story of the talent, the master chose them based on their abilities — five, three and one respectively. Aaron was a faithful lieutenant to Moses. Life has a way of giving us many opportunities and how we handle them makes the difference. Now let's talk about Moses, the one-talent man. It is believed that his Hebrew name might be — this is speculative — Immanuel, the God that tabernacle among us, because Jochebed and Amram and the whole of Israel were anticipating a messiah.

Moses and the servant who got one talent in the New Testament had some striking similarities. The latter felt it was not enough and never appreciated the privilege of being chosen by his master. Many people are like that. The servant's first instinct was to bury it. He dug the ground and hid his talent. Moses' parents also hid him for three months. But then, some things can neither be hidden nor destroyed. It might take a while for the dream to come through, but it shall surely come to pass. Although Moses represents one talent with a five-talent effort, he saved his generation after four hundred and thirty years. After forty years in the palace, he had to spend another forty years in Jethro's house, tending sheep and carrying on as nomadic. This man was to embark on on a rescue mission in the end Our method of training is opposed to God's method of education.

No man can hide you for a long time. Moses' mother could only keep him for ninety days. When the time is right, no man can stop you. You may be one-talent man or woman, you will rescue an entire generation with a five-talent effort.

Isolation: Joseph's Model

Joseph was gifted and loved by his father. Although his brothers didn't like him because of his dreams, God used him to save humanity. The day he announced to his brothers and the entire family the blueprint of God for his life, he was recruited to the I.S.O.L.A.T.I.O.N programme. His father observed the saying and sent him on an errand to feed his brothers.

> *And he dreamed yet another dream, and told it his brethren, and said, Behold, I have dreamed a dream more; and, behold, the sun and the moon and the eleven stars made obeisance to me. And he told it to his father, and to his brethren: and his father rebuked him, and said unto him, What is this dream that thou hast dreamed? Shall I and thy mother and thy brethren indeed come to bow down ourselves to thee to the earth? And his brethren envied him; but his father observed the saying.* **Genesis 37:9-11**

His father gave an exact interpretation of his dream after he had rebuked him. Here was someone who would be at the zenith of Egypt's economy, but the first place he started was to carry food to his brothers. You may be asked to carry out errands in life. These errands are not meant to humiliate or dishonour you but to stir the gift of God in you. Joseph's dreams could have led to pride in the average person. As soon as you tell your dreams to some people you, they will push you on your journey to greatness. The pathway to any form of greatness is a lonely. But the right people will set you up for greatness. Never disrespect those who aid your journey. Joseph was to be an errand boy to set his destiny in motion. There is no mean place to start in life. You may have started in an unknown world, but God only deploys it to usher you to the top.

Isolation: Jesus' Model

Never cut a tree down in the wintertime. Never make a negative decision in the low time. Never make your most important decisions when you are in your worst moods. Wait. Be patient. The storm will pass. The spring will come to. — Robert H. Schuller

Jesus is the express image of God. As matter of fact, he was God manifested in the flesh. Yet for thirty years, he was silent and never did any public ministration. He is the ultimate of God's power here on earth. He was born of an incorruptible seed and had a heavenly mandate but was buried in oblivion until the fullness of time. The day Adam and Eve sinned, Jesus was supposed to shed his blood for redemption, but it took four thousand years later for this to happen. Galatians 4:4 corroborates this — But when the fullness of the time was come, God sent forth his Son, made of a woman, made under the law.

In this timeline, God was working but no man ever saw or heard Him. All we know of was the prophetic utterance about him. The period of Jesus' ministry was amazing. What was he up to in 30 years? He never did a miracle and was never on any known record. He was in absolute obscurity but in the fullness of time, he was manifested. According to John 2:11, *"This beginning of miracles did Jesus in Cana of Galilee, and manifested forth his glory; his disciples believed on him."*

God set the time for the miracle ministry to begin, but Jesus the healer, the redeemer, the miracle worker was silent for almost thirty years. This is the principle of isolation. Many of us are capable of doing great in life, but the challenge is how to hold on to the right moment. Although you carry potential, God will isolate you to try and test you. This is where you are packaged and launched. If Jesus had to be silent for almost thirty years before the public ministry, don't despise your timeline.

ATTITUDE

"Your attitude determines your altitude in life."

Attitude is a way of thinking. It is an inward feeling expressed by behaviour. Even if you don't say a word, people can observe your attitude. Many people have lost great opportunities because of a poor attitude. Your attitude is an outward look based on your past experiences. It either attracts or repels people. One of the things I have learnt over the years is the importance of a great attitude towards life and people. When others don't see anything good in some people, I see the good in them.

An attitude is a library of your past, the present speaker, and a prophet of our future. It is the difference between failure and success. Many people are lacking in opportunities because of their laid-back attitude and laissez-faire lifestyle. The difference between successful and unsuccessful people is not money but attitude. Great and poor marriages are measured by attitude. It tells us what to expect in life and how far we can go. The secret to success is beyond the school you attended or the family you were born in; rather, it's in your attitude to where you are and where you want to go.

Your attitude will determine your success in all ramifications. It also determines your relationship with other people. I used to wonder why people leave the house of God. Then I realised that: 1% may leave due to death or an illness. 3% may move away from the vicinity, and 5% will quit due to the new relationships they make. Also, 9% leave because of spiritual reasons. 14% leave because they are not satisfied with the lifestyle of some people. Meanwhile, 68% quit because some church members' indifference to them.

If you treat people with importance, they will return the treatment. Your attitude can turn a problem into a blessing. Your attitude is not good because you are a Christian; it is not a button you turn on and off as you like. It must be on at all times. Regardless of what is going on in your life, your attitude can give you a competitive advantage. No one gets to the top without a winning attitude. You cannot control what happens to you, but you can manage your attitude to what happens to you. Similarly, you cannot control what others do to you, but you can control how you react to them. No amount of prescriptions can impact an attitude. Great opportunities can slip by if you have a poor attitude.

How Can You Develop A Winning Attitude?

1. People Sense Attitude.
Your attitude can make the difference in life. It will either be your greatest ally or an impediment. Your thoughts are like currents moving through the air. They can draw people to you or drive them away from you. God works on your attitude when you are in isolation. Great gifts and talents have been forfeited because of poor attitude. People will continue to lose out on opportunities unless they have the right attitude. A business may not succeed unless you believe in it. When it comes to

winning in life and moving to the top, your attitude can cause waves of impact. Don't allow a pessimistic or cynical attitude loiter around you. Human detectors usually detect lousy attitudes. Attitude can be likened to a piece of clothing stained with petrol. You perceive the smell, but you can't see it. This is how powerful your attitude is in life. People can sense a good and a rotten attitude.

2. Our Environment Constructs Our Attitude.

Babies do not choose their environment or family. But as they grow, they decide their attitude. A positive environment will have a positive impact on one's life. A negative one will also have a negative impact. Since you are a product of your environment, choose the domain that will aid your purpose in life. Don't let people poison your life and mire your attitude. This generation is bedevilled with the menace of peer pressure. Many have fallen for the borrowed culture of laziness. They have eliminated the idea that hard work creates success. It crept into the church and every facet of our lives. When I checked some immigrants living in Europe or the United States, I observed that the first generation was quite hard-working. They would work from morning to evening, from dawn to dusk. But if you look at their children and the next generation, you will notice a cultural shift. Unlike the previous generation, they are idle and lethargic.

Every man is a product of his environment. A man's life is relatively proportional to the influence of his surroundings. God will sometimes put you in an isolated environment to drill a great attitude in you. If you examine David's story, you might think it was cruel for his father to have sent him to look after the sheep alone. But on a closer examination, it's God excluding him in order to include him. God used the opportunity to work on his attitude. The expression on your face, your words, body language, work ethic, dressing and personality go a long way to construct your attitude.

3. Your Past is Irrelevant.

To get to the top, you need a winning attitude. And you must never build your future around your past. Jesus was born amid what could be termed a social stigma. His mother was pregnant out of wedlock, but He ignored the slander and never looked back. He never discussed his mother's situation and the mystery surrounding his birth. Nowhere in the Bible did he mention the circumstances that surrounded his birth.

You, too, can move beyond the scars of yesterday. Stop talking about your limited education. Stop advertising your pain. Stop repeating the stories of those who failed you. Rise above the tide of your past, and reach out to your future. Jesus overcame the stigma of a questionable background. David was probably a shameful son to his father, hence he was hidden at the backside of the wilderness. But then, God used the isolation to craft an unparalleled attitude destined for stardom. Moving to the top requires a fixation on the future ahead. You cannot always explain your past to your colleagues and competitors. When you have a winning attitude, your past becomes a springboard rather than a handbrake to your future.

4. Don't Waste Your Time on Faultfinders.

Critical people are usually depressed when they fail to reach a desired goal. They are disappointed, dissatisfied, disillusioned and frustrated people. They are hurting inside. As a result, they unleash their frustration on others. Don't be pressured to answer your critics. Remember, criticism points out your flaws, but correction reveals your potential. Faultfinders view the world with a negative lens, so I have decided not to allow any critic or whinger to determine my day.

Like Jesus Christ, we must learn to keep quiet at times. According to Matthew 26:63, "But Jesus kept silent. And the high priest said to Him, I call upon you to swear by the living God, and tell us whether you are the Christ, the Son of God." There are times in life when we need to hold onto our nerves in the face of critics. Sometimes when your ability or integrity is questioned, you must hold your peace. Your attitude can change independent of your environment and circumstances. But the more you allow a critic in your life, the longer it takes for the change to happen. When Jesus' mission was challenged, he held his peace. Learn from this. Don't spend too much time on people who cannot help you. A winning attitude demands a strong attitude. When David's brother questioned him, he held his nerves and said, "*...What have I now done? Is there not a cause? And he turned from him toward another, and spake after the same manner: and the people answered him again after the former manner* (1Samuel 17:29-30)".

God had earlier quarantined him and when the time came for him to be unveiled, he was ready. Sometimes, God will place you in an internship to model your resilience, confidence and conviction. If he had never responded to his brother in that manner before, that day was momentous for him. Similarly, we all have a particular day when we will break the yoke of pain off our necks.

5. Maintain the Right Attitude in Difficult Times.

Watch out for your emergencies; they are opportunities for divine intervention. At some point in life, the tide would be against you. But your attitude will be a powerful barging chip for success. Every future has two handles — anxiety and faith. In the face of trials, you need a faith-filled attitude. God sometimes takes us through great pain to strengthen our attitude. If you want to develop a winning attitude, you must maintain the right atmosphere and mindset. Today, many aspiring leaders don't know how to be calm in the face of challenges. Many will even quit at the slightest opposition to a project or a dream. If nobody is singing your praises today, always remember that the top is a lonely place, and you must be tough to get there. Having the right mood is crucial to success. When you find yourself in an obscure position, don't fret or complain because soon, the world will marvel at your abilities. David, according to 1 Samuel 18:14-15, *"acted wisely in all his ways and succeeded, and the Lord was with him. When Saul saw how capable and successful David was, he stood in awe of him."*

This is the testimony of David. Although he knew king Saul wanted him dead, he behaved himself more wisely, and the king was in awe of him. Many young pastors break camp from their main church and start their ministries down the road because their pastor reprimanded them. Many employees complain about their boss when they are corrected. David went through a lot in the hands of king Saul. He threw a spear at him twice, but he escaped. He even tricked him into marrying his daughter and demanded a dowry that would cost him his life. He sent him on errands aimed at eliminating him. Yet, in all of this, David behaved more wisely. And *"… David had more success and behaved himself more wisely than all Saul's servants, so that his name was very dear and highly esteemed."* (1 Samuel 18:30b)

David's attitude is in sharp contrast to what is typically associated with protégées. People have walked out of medical schools, Bible schools, universities and churches because they feel their superiors don't like them. But as long as you want to get to greater heights, maintain a healthy attitude even if you are being oppressed.

6. Never Judge People by Their Outward Appearance.

Packaging can be deceptive. To avoid deception, look out for people's attitudes and perceptions. Don't be deceived by appearances. One of the greatest assets in isolation is to learn how to package what you have. You must also realise that great things come in small packages. I have been misjudged many times because I did not meet the status quo in specific cycles. I was once in a meeting with other prominent men of God. The guest preacher was praying over people's lives. He came to where the pastors sat and started prophecy over every pastor. For reasons best known to him, he overlooked me and jumped to an elegant-looking pastor. I then noticed that these super-fit men of God had expensive shoes, costly watches, fanciful blazers and sophisticated cars. Because of who I am, I never got offended. I simply maintained a healthy attitude. Then the host introduced me to give some remarks and say the closing prayer. The preacher, who had earlier been oblivious to my presence, was amazed by my eloquence. As soon as we finished, he followed me to my car to take my number and wanted us to be friends.

God oftens isolates you to teach you how to accept unpleasant situations in life. Of course, the packaging is essential. Never judge people because they are not wearing a Giorgio Arman, Prada or polyester. Jesus saw beyond the adulterous woman. He saw her heart, a desire to change. She became the golden bridge that turned a whole town around. The Israelites saw Absalom's handsomeness, but he was a cold-blooded-killer! Be careful of how you measure people. David brought Jonathan's disabled son, Mephibosheth, to his royal table.

> *"So Mephibosheth dwelt in Jerusalem: for he did eat continually at the king's table; and was lame on both his feet."* **2 Samuel 9:13**

David did this to show favour to his long-standing friend. David had a great attitude towards packaging. When you have been poor and discounted before, you find it easy to help the needy. David never discriminated against Mephibosheth. Sadly in today's world, many gifted people are demoralised because of discrimination. Some are judged due to the pigment of their skin and the lack of a British accent, among other factors. Samson thought Delilah was the most beautiful woman, but she was the destructive and poisonous woman that brought him down. Moses had a speech impediment, yet he was the great statesman of his time. These examples are to show you that one must not judge people by their outward appearance. Learn to observe people's attitudes, thoughts, feelings and opinions. There is always more than meets the eye. A baby boy of today is a potential toddler, teenager, man, father, and grandfather. There is more in a person than you can see.

7. Avoid Unnecessary Confrontations.

Many have lost opportunities because they lingered in certain avoidable circumstances. Sometimes in life, you have to learn to walk away from confrontations. To some, flexing their muscles signifies status and significance. In the place of isolation, God keeps you until you are ready for the limelight. David's heroic deeds in the wilderness earned him bragging rights among his peers. But the Bible never mentioned that he bragged of his exploits. He gave due credit to God. His family didn't know about his conquest at the backside of the wilderness. He had a testimony but no one to tell. In the earlier days of my ministry, no one wanted to hear my exploits from my time as the senior prefect in the Bible college. It was the most fantastic experience of my life yet nobody, not even my family, wanted to know the wonderful way in which God had used me. But God, over the years, has taught me to walk away from people who want to undermine my ability.

As noted earlier, David had been trained in the art of war behind closed doors. But when he came to the battlefield, his brother confronted and undermined him (1 Samuel 17:28). He could have bragged about his triumph in the wilderness, but he held his peace. At some point in life, you will be given the stage to fight back and retaliate. But for every success in your life, your attitude is as important as your ability. This is why you spend a long time at the backside of the wilderness to create a winning attitude. And remember, excellence is not a gift but an attitude.

8. Your Mindset is the Administrator of Your Actions.

Negative thoughts produce negative actions, and positive thoughts produce positive actions. We are where we are and what we are because of the thoughts that dominate our minds. Your mindset is the superintendent of your actions in life. This is why you become what you hear constantly. If you feed your mind on negativity, your life would be filled with negativity. No man is greater than his mindset.

The Effects of a Negative Mindset

- **It Creates Negativity During Critical Decisions.**

Most of us have been affected by a negative mindset. It is the cancer of the soul. It syphons hope and optimism from a vision. The most brilliant idea conceived in a negative mindset will result in abortion. A negative mindset precipitates doom and gloom. God uses isolation to erase the pile of inferiority complex and negative perspectives in us. This is why professional athletes and footballers set camps far away from family, friends and foes to remove negative mindsets.

- **It is Infectious.**

A negative mindset is like a contagious disease. Pessimistic and misanthropic parents will eventually produce a sardonic child because children are shaped by the actions of their parents. My greatest prayer is that you don't let a negative mindset linger around you and your family. Let your experiences contribute to your success. When failure precedes success, it removes the mindset of "I can't do it" to "yes, I can!"

- **It Blows Situations out of Proportion.**

If your thought process is negatively programmed, your life will be out of control. A negative mindset is as mighty as weapons of mass destruction. Don't allow a negative mindset to endanger your life. You have been given a sound mind and a renewed mindset (2 Timothy 1:7). A negative mindset opens you up to the most devastating dilemma in life. Never start any profitable venture with negative thinking; it will be disastrous. Avoid negativity at all times.

- **It Puts Breaks on God and Your Potential.**

God can't use someone with a negative mindset. In life, your ability is tied to your mindset. If you think you can, you can! But when you think you cannot, it would be difficult to make you do what your mind has concluded it cannot do. In times of isolation, God performs a massive overhauling of your mindset. Moving from being a shepherd boy to a king has to do with the right mindset. Moving from a poor boy to becoming the leader of a nation is a function of the mindset. If you can conceive, you can receive it.

- **It Keeps Us From Enjoying Life.**

The mind is an incredible tool God has given us. During one of our morning devotions, I explained the power of the mind to my children. We have over two hundred apps on our smart TV, but they only use three — YouTube, Amazon prime and Netflix. Other apps remain untapped. They cannot know the capacity of the remaining apps except when they tap into them. Our mindset is oftentimes enclosed in a negative orientation because we fail to look beyond the negative just as my children only focus on three apps. Consequently, a negative mindset prevents us from enjoying the simple things of life. You must step out of the box of negative thinking.

- **It Hinders Others From Giving Us Positive Responses.**

When you are negatively programmed, you repel your helpers. A mindset full of negativity can't attract the best in life. If you are a leader, your greatest asset is the feedback of your subordinates. But if you are a negative leader, it becomes difficult for them to give you a positive response. How you react to your associates sometimes reflects on your success. The most successful people are not always the most educated or talented. But they have quality people who are willing to die for them because of their attitude. When you are in isolation, God shapes your attitude to embrace humility when you become successful.

THRIVING

What would you attempt to do if you knew you would not fail?
- Robert Schuller

To thrive is to be successful. It also means growing vigorously; flourishing and prospering. It is a state of healthy growth mainly because the conditions are right. A thriving Christian prospers in his or her undertakings (Psalms 92:13-14). Such Christians are capable of facing challenges without relinquishing their integrity and honour. They are planted where they labour patiently. They pay attention to their calling. Flowers do not grow merely to satisfy ambitions or to fulfil good intentions. They thrive because someone put in an effort to cultivate them. Never underestimate isolation; it is the foundation for thriving in life.

A thriving Christian is someone who depends solely on God's word, someone who relies on the Holy Spirit. All the characters of the Bible who made it to the hall of fame in Hebrews thrived. They depended on God and learnt to succeed even in unpleasant circumstances. That you are thriving does not mean you will not experience defeats or disappointment. But you must not allow these stumbling blocks to stop you from serving God.

Just as Joseph did, a thriving Christian sees every challenge as an opportunity to serve God and glorify Him. Addressing his brothers in Genesis 50:20, Joseph said *"But as for you, ye thought evil against me; but God meant it unto good, to bring to pass, as it is this day, to save much people alive."* When life throws bricks at a thriving Christian, he lays a firm foundation with them. The difference between a thriving Christian and others is not a lack of strength but a lack of will and motivation.

When I published my first book, it came out better than I anticipated because I had developed my gift in isolation. Many want to succeed, but they have refused to thrive in the lean season of their lives. If you observe the major players in the Bible, you will discover that they thrived in isolation before they were brought to limelight. They were men and women that flourished in the most austere circumstances.

When you are in isolation where no one considers you capable, don't be discouraged. Learn to thrive when no one applauds or acknowledges you. In the church I pastor, our prayer meetings and weekday services are often discouraging in the winter. But I thrive in this kind of meeting because I was once a leader of a house fellowship when I was in Ghana. I would prepare for the prayer meeting and bible study, but no one would show up. I would preach to the empty building and end the service as though the fifteen to twenty members were there. I endured those days when no one encouraged me. I learnt to pat myself on the back while walking down the street. I never blamed anybody nor the environment. Despite the disappointment, I would still look forward to the following Monday's meeting. I refused to give in to discouragement because people did not determine my success. My success was based on my determination and consistency.

Many people are looking for accreditation even before they start a project. In isolation, you must learn to cry, congratulate and encourage yourself. It would be best if you can come back to do it all over again without an iota of disappointment or bitterness. This attitude makes you dogged as you pursue your goals. Before David killed Goliath, he had killed a lion and bear. Before Moses led Israel out of slavery to the promised land, he had to graze his father-in-law's sheep alone in the desert. Joseph was imprisoned before becoming a prime minister in Egypt. You will cry on some days and wish the world would stand to cheer you. But as long as you persevere, your critics will celebrate you.

The Ten Powerful Signs of a Thriving Life

1. Stability: Your stability determines how long you will last at the top. Remember, commitment is a continuous process, not a coincidence. It is not how fast you go in life but how far you can go. Also, in a marathon, it is not how quickly you can run but how stable you are in the race.

2. Perseverance: Thriving people pursue their goals with determination and fortitude. You cannot be at the top without perseverance. You cannot be in your lazy boy chair and be persevering. Someone once said, "The road to success is dotted with many tempting parking places". You must be resolute if you desire to reach the pinnacle in life. Nothing comes on a silver platter. You must be a stubborn person as you pursue your purpose. Perseverance is a stepping stone to the top. You cannot reach the zenith of life without the ingredient of determination.

3. Resourcefulness: Those who thrive in life believe that God has given them the necessary resources to fulfil their assignment. They are also creative and inventive. They stay on top of their game because of their resourcefulness. They turn businesses around and make profit. If you give them one gift, they multiply it. A thriving person will take what you underestimate and turn it into a multimillion-dollar business. Some people have just a talent, but their resourcefulness lies in their ability to diversify. So they will continue to thrive where others fail.

4. Faith in God: Faith is a strong conviction, a firm belief in something for which there may be no tangible proof. It is a complete trust in God. Isolation teaches you that you have an anchor that keeps the soul. It is steadfast and sure when the billows roll. Isolation makes your faith unshakeable. Faith is your "magic" card in life. Some people's entire life is based on guesswork because their faith has not been tried. There's no natural substance to what they say or do in life. In isolation, you learn to walk by faith and grow in it. When you get stuff easily, your faith becomes underdeveloped. Faith has exploits; it can move the unseen to the visibility realm. Faith makes it possible to move intangible things to the realm of possibility. Faith is the thread that connects the abstract to reality. Faith can disable unbelief; it can also remove impossibilities. Consequently, a thriving man or woman possesses a strong faith.

5. They Look Beyond Adversity: In every adversity, there is an equivalent amount of advantage. A thriving person doesn't allow today's adversity to hamper tomorrow's testimony. When you look beyond adversity, you become an institution of learning. Many of the great men and women we emulate learnt to look beyond their misfortunes and see a new horizon. You have a great future if you can see beyond your present predicament. Some people will judge you today, but you must see yourself in the tomorrow you spoke about yesterday. Never allow your today to misjudge your tomorrow. You must understand that today isn't the end of life. There is always another day to try again. God told Abraham he was going to be the father of many nations. He did not understand the revelation, so God told him to come out of the tent and see beyond the four corners. Your current situation is not the conclusion. It is just the process. And the God of the process is the God of the outcome.

6. Motivation: Those who thrive are not easily discouraged or depressed by other people's triumphs. Never allow someone's success to be your aspiration, but let it be your inspiration. There's a tiny line between arrogance and confidence in your ability. Sometimes, when people are motivated, we think they are arrogant or complacent. I have met young people who think they can change the world, so they describe their predecessors' ideas as myopic. While motivation is a good thing, one must be careful. Life is engineered to dwarf your spirit, at times you, but you must motivate yourself. Motivated people know when to abase and abound. That you are motivated does not give you the right to humiliate others around you or make them feel inadequate. In your efforts to embrace motivation, never crush other people.

7. Spiritual Discipline: Thriving people are prayerful; they are committed and faithful members of a church. Spiritual discipline opens the heavens and activates favour. Many 21st century success books omit this important factor. To be spiritually disciplined is more than being religious. In my line of duty, many people only commit to spiritual discipline when they want something from God. They are only spiritual if they need divine assistance. A thriving person is not seasonal when it comes to trusting in God. They see God as a pivot of their success in life. As you prepare for the top, make spirituality your anchor.

8. They Are Potential Givers: Thriving people are faithful stewards; they are great custodians of divine resources. They are not stingy either. Someone said to be rich is to be able to reach out to other people. I once watched a funny video on social media platforms. This guy went around doing a social experiment. He went past some homeless people and intentionally dropped his wallet to see if they would take it or not. Out of about ten homeless people, eight called his attention to his wallet. He did the same experiment on a street with professionals and well-to-dos. Nobody called his attention. Life is about giving because potential givers are potential lifesavers. Every thriving person knows how to give and can reach out to others with riches. It doesn't matter how poor or rich you are right now, make it a duty to be a giver.

9. Determination To Finish Well: Thriving people are not quitters. Once they start a thing, they must end it. Some people started well but became discouraged when the race got tough. Thriving people start with grit, and they finish the race with the same attitude. Some great talents fizzle out along the road of trials and temptations. Those at the cutting edge of any endeavour started and finished with determination. Some people are easily discouraged, so they blame others. But it takes a strong mind to overcome any stronghold in life. You can't be emotionally unstable and still be on top of the game. You have to be determined in the face of challenges.

10. A significant Vision: Regardless of their age or financial status, thriving people have a big vision. Having a bigger vision is not a shortcut to stardom. And anything you can do for yourself is no longer a vision. A vision is a mental picture of the future you talked about yesterday. It is the power of the unseen brought into reality. Thriving people have larger than life visions. They might look small, but they have a great vision. Thriving people always have something more prominent than their capacity.

How Do You Cultivate a Thriving Life in Isolation?

1. Be Intentional.

To cultivate a thriving lifestyle, you must be intentional. Live with a purpose as well as a determination to succeed. No master plan in life can deliver instant success. Success does not happen without being intentional. And intentionality does not by accident or error. Getting to the top requires lots of deliberate actions. Excellence is deliberate, and winning is a premeditated phenomenon. Being intentional increases your chances of succeeding and being at the top. David proceeded to the battlefield with an intention (1 Samuel 17). His dialogue with King Saul and the choice of the armoury was intentional. His attitude towards the selection of his weapons was deliberate. He chose five stones, not six, not twelve or eight. His choice of words with Goliath was intentional. If you want to get to the top, you must take deliberate actions.

2. Give Yourself to Thriving.

Give, and it shall be given unto you; good measure, pressed down, and shaken together, and running over, shall men give into your bosom. For with the same measure that ye mete withal, it shall be measured to you again. (Luke 6:38)

I can't play musical instruments because I have not given myself to them. The above passage says give, which means to be committed and devoted, because it is rewarding. If you see someone doing something so well, they have given themselves to learning. I love children's day in our church, especially when they are reciting some memory verses. You would see an unassuming child putting a Bible passage together and speaking fluently. This is proof that we can all give ourselves something. I have had the opportunity to spend time in church as a member, a leader, a youth leader, home-cell leader, a branch pastor and now a founder of a ministry. In all my developmental stages, I gave myself to thriving. It began as an unintended action, but I understood the principle eventually. If you diligently give yourself to something in life, it will return to you in good measure.

3. Have Faith In God.

A thriving Christian walks by faith, not by sight. No one thrives in life without walking by faith. One person with faith is equal to a force of ninety-nine who have only interests. Faith is the key that unlocks the door of impossibilities. It means you trust God to fulfill His promise. It is the act of putting a demand on the integrity of the word of God. It is a demonstration of your confidence in God. Faith takes the first step even when you don't see the whole staircase. Keep driving to church, keep serving that mean manager, keep sowing seeds, keep running errands for the pastor, and keep serving in that church. With faith, the doors of opportunities will open to you. It is said that "Millions of trees in the world are accidentally planted by squirrels, who bury nuts, then forget where they hid them. Do good and forget. It will grow someday."

David demonstrated his faith in 1 Samuel 17:45. He said to Goliath: *"Thou comest to me with a sword, and with a spear, and with a shield: but I come to thee in the name of the LORD of hosts, the God of the armies of Israel, whom thou hast defied."* This is faith in its fullest proportion. What gave a seventeen-year-old boy this kind of courage? The experienced soldiers were running for cover, but a teenager faced the giant with faith. Faith allows excellent things to happen. It is the power that comes from a courageous and gallant heart. You may not have much to go on with today. But remember that absolute trust in God is the greatest lesson you can learn in isolation. A tested faith is a proven faith. And you can only kill a giant if you have killed your bear and your lion.

4. Have a Winning Mindset.

Every potential leader must have a winning mindset. It will never be handed over to you over the counter at your local shop or in the post by a TV evangelist. It is helpful to cultivate a winning mindset when you are in isolation. When life pushes you down the ladder, look beyond your present state. The state of your mind determines your chances of winning a battle. The strength of your mind is determined by the amount of God's word it has experienced. It's not the length of life that matters but the depth of life. And the deeper the depth, the stronger the mindset.

David knew Goliath was no match for him. But he had a winning attitude. He looked beyond his opponent's size. It is widely quoted that if your mind can conceive something, your hands can receive it. Think like a winner. Although having a winning mentality does not happen overnight, it is a process. To move to the top, you must have the attitude of a winner.

5. Have a Tenacious Attitude.

A thriving person is someone willing to go beyond their comfort zone. If we are to go beyond our comfort zone, we will break a record. That something didn't work out the first time doesn't mean it is over. A stagnant lifestyle is fuelled by blame culture and refusal to take responsibility because nobody is willing to help us. Do you want to succeed? How steadfast are you? Most essential things in the world today have been accomplished by people who kept on trying when there seemed to be no hope at all (Dale Carnegie).

Tenacity cannot be overlooked when training for any great accomplishment in life. There are no secret manuals to success anywhere. It is mainly the by-product of persistence, sagacity and tenacity. If I count how many times I was turned down in life and ministry, you will be amazed. But it spurred me on to greater heights. Despite the agony, the joy of waking up in the morning to try again kept me going. David's story always amazes me. What if, when the brother reprimanded him, he got offended and went home? Many people left their churches, jobs and even marriages because somebody questioned their motives. When time and chance collide with tenacity, triumph is immediate. And remember that great people are ordinary people with tenacity.

INFLUENCE

Power may last at least ten years, but influence can outlive you for a century.

Influence is the capacity to affect the character, development or behaviour of someone or something. Influence is like perfume. It can wear off, so you must keep it alive. Power may last for ten years, but influence can outlive you. When God isolates you, He deposits a certain level of influence in you. The foundation of an extraordinary life is built on integrity and influence. Influence isn't created in a day or a year. It is made in a lifetime. And it differentiates great leaders from ordinary ones. Anytime God places you in isolation, he builds your influence.

John Maxwell wrote: "Leadership is influence. Nothing more, nothing less." Webster's dictionary defines influence as "the capacity or power of persons or things to be a compelling force on or produce effects on the actions, behaviour, opinions, etc., of others." For me, influence is the ability to make others do the impossible, bring out the best in others and create an environment for talents to thrive. Great people are influenced by certain people, and they will eventually influence others. People spend thousands of pounds learning to be charming in public. That is influence. It is the ability to attract attention and make an impact in your domain.

Influence can be likened to the word "Doma". It means domicile or domain. Doma is an official documentation that defines a sphere of administrative authority or control within a network. Domicile is related to a space or a territory, your legal place to function. And it comes with power and influence. Your domain can be stolen; it can also malfunction. Some gifted individuals lack influence because their "domicile" has been compromised. Influence is the hidden factor God puts in a gifted person. The word "celebrity" is a product of influence.

Although influence can be cultivated, God can bestow it on a person in the grand scheme of things. Haven't you met someone you don't know but something draws you to them? You just enjoy hearing them speak. One day, my last born heard Joel Osteen speaking, and he asked me about his name. When I told him, he said, "I like him". He went on to add: "there's something about the way he speaks". This was a thirteen-year-old British-born. Since he was born, he has heard only a few Sunday school teachers and his father, a hard-punching preacher. He listened to this sound and lovely preacher for about three to five minutes, and he fell in love with the voice and mode of presentation. This is the power of influence. What money and threats cannot achieve, influence accomplishes in seconds. Influence convicts the heart in minutes.

Influence is the ingredient that your education cannot give. What makes your mentor or tutor great is not good dressing and expensive cars; it is influence. Influence causes either a positive or negative response. God commands you to be a positive influence.

Five Kinds of Influence:

1. Natural Influence

This type of influence neither adds to nor subtracts from your life. People with this influence don't add value to your life. They are people who have lost weight in your life. They are light-coloured when it comes to your progress. They are people who don't matter but, for some reason, are still part of your journey. Natural influencers may have helped you initially, but as you grow, they lose essence and value. Parents influence their children at the early stages of their lives, but as they become adults, other forms of influence come up. This is because times have changed, and their friends mean more than parents' opinions. It doesn't mean they don't love or respect their parents; they only find their worldview different from theirs. As such, your influence in their lives declines.

2. Negative Influence

Earlier, I noted how my thirteen-year-old boy heard Joel Osteen talk and fell in love with the smooth-talker preacher. What if he had a negative vibe? Who is influencing your child? Many people in authority sway the younger generation with negative actions. Today's world is filled with men and women with bad influence. A negative influencer is full of pride; he gives nothing but bad vibes. Some good people have lost their lives to bad influences. If you want to have a lasting impact in life, you must run away from negative influences.

3. Positive Influence

Positive influencers are golden links that ensure you walk in the right direction. This generation lacks people who will positively influence the next generation. A positive influencer adds value to lives. And God builds such people in isolation. Your ability to effect a change in people's lives depends on how much impact you have acquired. There's a level of freedom and expertise you attain as a result of training. This is the reason for isolation — to groom you and move you to the next level. And positive influence comes with intentionality.

4. Demonic Influence

Demonic influence is triggered by a sinister force. Sometimes, people are influenced to do things they would never do normally. The modern-day music, social media, gambling, pornography and influx of video games are all geared towards influencing the next generation. We are brainwashed to embrace demonic activities. Modern-day witchcraft is intrusive. Those who are demonically influenced have the power to manipulate lives. And our world has embraced influencers with demonic attributes. They function in a realm of power; they control the masses. They influence trends, fashion, and social media. What they say, do and promote become widely accepted. There's a new trend called predicted programming. From children-targeted movies (cartoons) to the giant Hollywood billboards of movies, soap operas and the like, everything is part of a more extensive agenda. The agenda is to sway people to have a certain mindset. This is the dynamics of influence; it's either godly (positive) or ungodly (demonic). The world needs to eliminate influencers who are a conduit for evil. Consequently, we must raise a godly generation to counter the demonic systems of the world.

5. Godly Influence

Godly influence is sometimes unexplainable. Any man or woman who has had an experience with God in the secret place carries such an influence. It is said that "the baker smells like the bakery; the pharmacist smells like pharmaceuticals." Similarly, if you spend time with God, you will smell like Him.

Moses was there with the Lord forty days and forty nights ...When Moses came down from Mount Sinai with the two tablets of the Testimony in his hand, he did not know that the skin of his face was shining [with a unique radiance] because he had been speaking with God. When Aaron and all the Israelites saw Moses, behold, the skin of his face shone, and they were afraid to approach him. (Exodus 34:28a-30, AMP)

The phrase, "with a unique radiance" connotes exceptionality and exclusivity. Godly influence can only be acquired in a secret place. If you spend time in the secret place of God, you have a deposit of His power, presence and unction. Sometimes, people spend too long in God's incubator, and we wonder why. The strength of a building is not in the beauty but in the unseen foundation. The longevity of a building is not in the finishing but in the foundation. When you spend time in God's lab of isolation, your influence increases. Don't get tired in the secret place because God is preparing you for greatness. Your influence is relatively proportional to your preparation. Preparation is hard work, but it's worth the wait.

Keycodes To Influence

These are means through which you can derive influence. They include:

1. Keycode of Association

Influence does not work in a vacuum. It has a source. In every field of life, we have those we emulate from how we dress to how we cook. These are the codes of influence. This is why medical students understudy other doctors. In life, we observe others so we can learn from them. No matter who you are, someone influenced you. Association is a porter for the transference of gifts and ideas. The power you associate with can make or unmake you. Many youths have been derailed by their peers. This shows that whoever you move with will eventually impact your life. We are what we constantly associate with. Your cooking skills, for instance, are not far from your mother's because we learn what we know. You didn't just become a bank manager or a mechanic. You were never born a chef. Someone would have influenced you at some point.

Sometimes, when I go to the bank, I would see a banker looking over the shoulders of the bank teller. I used to think they were watching for fraudulence. But they are there to be trained. Association brings transformation. Jesus associated with the disciples for three years, and they were transformed. The Scribes and Sanhedrin were amazed that these uneducated men could communicate on a level beyond their understanding. Anytime you associate with a gift or a greater dimension, it rubs off on you.

> *Now when the men of the Sanhedrin (Jewish High Court) saw the confidence and boldness of Peter and John and grasped the fact that they were uneducated and untrained [ordinary]*

men, they were astounded and began to recognise that they had been with Jesus.
Acts 4:13 AMP

Moses had to raise Joshua, Elijah raised Elisha, and Jesus raised the disciples. These men were influenced based on their association. Our children don't listen to what we say; they watch what we do. You are an influencer in your home. The power to transfer knowledge and skills is in your hands. Your greatest gift on earth is not the material wealth you leave behind but your influence on the next generation. Your gift will fade, but your result will never expire.

2. Keycode of Service

There's a keycode that makes people receive from those they render services to. In today's world, we are urged to never be a fool for anyone. The "Yes, you can generation!" While there is a place for that, we must remember that life is based on a principle. Methods can change, but principles must be adhered to. There's no great leader who was not a great servant. If you aim to get to the top, never rebuff servant(ship) because you become what you yield to. You can only be given what you are willing to die for.

Your lifeline to the top is service, which is a keycode to unlock the future. When you are willing to stoop for people, your generation will stand for you. The most significant seed you can sow on earth is the seed of service. People may remember you for many things; one of the things time never forgets is service. Whoever you serve in life deposits part of themselves in you. You may say, "I don't look or think like them", but you have covertly carried an influence. Many pastors who served under certain great men of God may not sound like their leaders but if you look closely, there is a measure of influence on them.

3. Keycode of Bequeathment

The word bequeath can be likened to an inheritance. Some doors will open for you because of who your master or leader is. When I tell people who my pastor is, doors are open. This is the power of influence. As soon as they know who I am, opportunities and doors are open to me. Some names in our generation will enjoy perpetual joy and breakthroughs because of influence. When the Sanhedrin saw the boldness of Peter and John, they perceived they had been with Jesus (Acts 4:13). "Katalambano" is the Greek word for perceived, which means "to apprehend, attain, come upon and become aware or conscious of something; to come to realise or understand". Until now, we are not known in the corridors of power because we never rendered services and never spent time in the place of preparation. You must be connected to a person of influence before you are given what is due to you. Moses was a deliverer, but he was connected to Jethro. Why? Through Jethro, a great statesman was born, and the idea of governance came to be. Anyone with a significant influence had somebody bequeath it to them.

Influence can be given to you like an inheritance. Because Jesus walked with the disciples, they received a transferred influence. The church inherited a name that is above any other title on earth. Every knee bows, and demons tremble before this name. It is bequeathed, and it works on any level of life. When you say you are a Christian, it is a statement of fact that it was given to you by God through His son, Jesus. Your name will never cure a fly or cast a spell but when you employ the name of Jesus, you command influence. I was given a first-class ticket when the flight attendant realised I was a reverend minister. I have been trusted with privileged information when people learnt I was a man of God. Doors that my natural name cannot open have opened because of the name I bear as a child of God. Jesus died two thousand years ago and has given us a name. Whatever we demand in the name will be done for us. This is the epitome of influence.

4. Keycode of Transfer

Transfer in today's world is synonymous with money or currency. It is the "power to assign, allocate or transmit". Without the keycode of transfer of influence, we would never have heard of certain people. The most outstanding example is Joel Osteen. I greatly admire this man of God because I know of his father as a preacher. Of course, he worked hard because of the magnitude of the level of ministry now, but his father transferred a level of influence to him. There are specific names in the faith today that carry influence. Oral Roberts is believed to have received a transfer of anointing from Kathryn Kuhlman.

Brands, products and territories have had

influence transferred to them. Certain products will be the most valuable in the marketplace compared to similar products. Over the years, Sony, Philips and Apple have been allocated prestige. Adidas and Calvin Klein have some amount of prominence in life in the fashion business because of transferred influence. It is associated with something great and some amount of integrity. Certain gifted people may not make it to the top because they lack influence. The day your nation's president wears your product, it gains eminence. The day your manager or pastor wears your creation, it has a transferred reputation. Why do we advertise products with celebrities? Why do renowned actors and celebrities promote brands? It's called shared influence.

Whenever God hides you, He is preparing an influence to catapult you to your next level. David was unveiled by a transferred influence, the prophet Samuel. Jesus was revealed by a renowned preacher, John the Baptist. The apostles rubbed shoulders with the powers of their days because of Jesus' influence. In isolation, God prepares a transferred influence as a springboard to lift you. He sends some people your way to change your life. You will be seen with specific "big shots" that will revolutionise your life. They are high-powered delegates to bridge the gap between your present and future.

5. Keycode of Cultivation

You may not have the opportunity to access transferred influence, so you have to do the hard work. You cultivate it with patience and calculated precession. Cultivation requires growth, planting, ploughing, and watching. God isolates you to cultivate your reputation as an outstanding businesswoman by making you manage your mum's coffee shop. Your ability to do the hard work without grumbling is a form of cultivated influence. There is a fantastic story in the Bible where king Jehoshaphat said, *"Is there not here a prophet of the LORD that we may enquire of the LORD by him?"* (2 Kings 3:11a) We did not know much about Elisha, but he had built an influence in his local territory. The second part of that verse says, *"And one of the kings of Israel's servants answered and said, Here is Elisha the son of Shaphat, which poured water on the hands of Elijah."*

Influence can be cultivated just like anything in life. For years, Elisha poured water into the hands of his master, Elijah. The only reason the king trusted Elisha, deeming him fit to be a man of integrity, was not because of his accolades as a prophet. He trusted him because of what he had grown over the years. He had cultivated something most of this generation lacked by pouring water on Elijah's hands. If Elisha was to have signage to his church or business, it would have read, "Elisha, the prophet, trained by Elijah". This is an influence, and it can be grown over the years. Some grow it but are in so much of a hurry and harvest it too soon. Others are like the older brother of the prodigal son. They stayed too long and may have grieved themselves of timing.

In the UK, sometimes I see specific products struggle to advance in terms of success and prosperity. Yet others thrive. The difference is the cultivation of integrity and good practice. Cars and gadgets like vacuum cleaners, when sold by specific names or people, make it into every household. Others would have to struggle and may disappear after a period. The difference is that one took time to cultivate while the other left it to chance.

6. Keycode of Innate Influence

Some people are naturally gifted with some of the things others struggle with. Some people are just likeable while others are not. You may not know them closely, but there is this aura about them that makes you like them. I was once in a school with a young man who was dubious in his dealings when you got close to him. Yet you will fall in love with him the first day you meet him. You will just like people like him; they don't need to work on their smile, body language or mannerism. He is the kind of person you need at your front desk to be the face of the company. He could speak and dress well, and he came across as a charming person. There are people like that in our world who are just perfect for the atmosphere.

Regarding Moses, Exodus 2:2 (MSG) says, *"…The woman became pregnant and had a son. She saw there was something special about him and hid him."* When he was born, there was a custodial sentence of death on his life. His family took a risk by hiding him in the house for ninety days. The KJV of the verse says, *"… and when she saw him that he was a goodly child"*. Moses had something that made his parents risk their lives to hide him. It was said that Moses glowed in the dark. He was called a "goodly" child. The word goodly is "tobe" in Hebrew, which means pleasant, precious, favour, sweet and joyful.

Moses arrived on earth with a special glow that gave him influence. This kid wouldn't need you to talk on his behalf. He was that kid whose looks opened doors. He had it from birth, and his innate influence made a way for him. Anytime you find yourself in isolation, God is working on your influence. This is why we need to trust God. People might not know you today, but believe God to galvanise you with influence. When Moses spent forty years in isolation, what was deposited in him came forth. Life is a matter of contact and connections. In isolation, the reality of who you are is revealed. During this time, God connects you with those who will bring the best out of you.

ORDER

When you see order, it is the repetition of pieces of things together, whereas chaos is multiple things without rhythm.

God is not confined to working only with an order. God can bring light out of darkness and harmony out of discord. God uses certain ways to get order out of chaos in a place of isolation. The revelation of "isolation" was the epitome of my life when I was a young preacher. I learnt many things that people admire in my life today. At the time, it was scary. My upbringing was below average, but I stood out from the crowd with a bit of order and organisation. I lived about two hours away from the church I attended then. I was the one to start the meetings with an opening prayer. The service would begin at about 8.00 am. This is what order in isolation means; I was in that church for sixteen years and was never late for any service. How did I do it? Order, organisation and optimisation!

Many top-level officials are halted by disorder. A degree or college education can take you to the top, but lack of ethics and an organised lifestyle in addition to indiscipline can destroy your life beyond recognition. Hard work pays, but we must be disciplined. An order may not be seen, but disorder is recognisable. Therefore, when you find yourself in the dungeons of life and you are shut away from the everyday lifestyle, your best product should be order, organisation and optimisation. What is an order? In defining order, let's look at this scenario. Have you ever tried to use a lift or a toilet and you see the sign out of order? How did you feel when you saw the sign? Our churches, marriages, homes, and even governments are out of order in this generation. The whole of society has been out of order for a long time.

Order is the arrangement or disposition of people or things about each other according to a particular sequence, pattern, or method. The Cambridge Dictionary defines it as "the state of working correctly or being suitable for use". My definition of O.R.D.E.R is: being organised, rendered to a system or process, dedicated to something without wavering, having established set patterns, and being regulated to fit in any mould in life.

O: Organised
R: Rendered
D: Dedicated
E: Established
R: Regulated

I believe God is raising a new generation of men and women to the top, and they need to maximise their potential. Order and organisation are not bought from the shop. No amount of prayer meetings will impute order in your life. Just reading about it won't solve the problem. You must cultivate the habit. Turning up on time for a meeting should not be spiritualised or seen as eccentricity. Punctuality and obedience to instructions, among others, shouldn't be seen as mediaeval practices. Many young men and women keep failing because they are out of order. They play the card of ignorance and make unfounded excuses in life. Order is the state of working correctly or being eligible for use. When God places you in isolation, He wants you to be in O.R.D.E.R.

Order is Organisation

Organise means to "arrange into a structured whole; order, coordinate and manage." An organised person is a recognised person. See a man diligent in his business, and he will not stand before mean men. David rose to the top of the army because he acted wisely. This is where most of us miss it. You have not been promoted not because you didn't qualify, or you are not cut for the job, but sometimes you don't act wisely. I invited somebody to speak at our church's conference some time ago. He came in late and even exceeded the time allotted to him. He was overtly disrespectful to the ministry. Acting wisely is more than being friendly and polite. When God prunes you in a place of isolation, you come out well structured. You may be uneducated, but when God isolates you, you emerge as a structured whole. You become organised too.

Earlier, I mentioned how I was punctual to church service when I was young. Service would start at 8.00 am, and I needed to be there before then. What time did I leave home? How did I put myself together for the service? This is where organisation comes in. How you organise your time, money and resources is important for the future. Some young pastors want the top job but can't organise the few people in their care. You can't land the big time if you can't handle the small time entrusted to you. Organise your time, put yourself in order and be in control of yourself before you control others. There are too many aspirants without training and too many contenders without attendants. If you don't get the training in isolation when an opportunity comes, you will falter.

> *Therefore, when Saul saw that he behaved very wisely, he was afraid of him*
> **1 Samuel 18:15**

Some people would criticise everybody but once you give them a chance, they fumble. Life is not as easy as we think. Now that no one knows you, behave wisely. Act tactfully. Be like David who "when Saul saw that he behaved very wisely, he was afraid of him (1 Samuel 18:15). King Saul wanted him dead, yet David never said a negative word. Stretch yourself in this manner, so that you can be fit for that position you have always wanted. The people who get to the top are those who are organised.

Order is Rendered

To render in this context is to "provide or give (a service, help, etc.), depict a picture, submit to."

In isolation, you learn to submit yourself to authority; you also become disciplined. If you don't render anything, you cannot demand anything from life. In your isolation, learn to control your appetite. Give yourself to studying, and submit to self-control. Many people have to deal with 'extras' in life because when nobody knew them, they never gave themselves to good practices. What is in you will eventually come out when you come under pressure. If you serve in a church as an associate, never allow your senior pastor or Bishop to be in church before you. Render yourself to a high level of discipline.

When you are given the time slot to preach or speak in a place, respect your host and audience. Be orderly wherever you find yourself. Never take any opportunity for granted.

Proverbs 24:10 (MSG) says, *"If you fall to pieces in a crisis, there wasn't much to you in the first place."* Some people will curve in at the verge of greatness. Life's scanner will reveal what's in you. And some of the things you desire will only come out at the centre stage of your opportunity. Stop hiding behind spirituality. Stop inflating your ego too. Humble yourself in order to learn. If you are lacking in any area, devote your time to learning. Never fall into pieces on the day of your opportunity. Learn to do a presentation, learn to teach, and learn to speak correctly. Depict a picture your leader will be proud of and learn to do things well. Don't leave things to chance in the name of spirituality because anything you yield to in life will reward you.

Order is Dedication

Dedication implies devoting time, effort or oneself to a particular task or purpose. Your success in life is dependent on your commitment to your goals. And regardless of the outcome, you will be glad that you gave it your best. Only a few people are willing to dedicate themselves to their gift. I was privileged to be in isolation most of my adult life. I dedicated myself to studies and the act of preaching. As far back as 1986, when I was a newspaper vendor on the streets of Accra, I knew I was going to be a speaker someday. Then in school, I always read in the class or gave a speech on prize-giving days. So, when I took my portion of the newspaper from my Mum, I had a notepad in my back pocket to jot new words, phrases and quotes.

There has never been a day I never learnt something new all through my life. Dedicate yourself to learning. Many so-called leaders refuse to be dedicated. Hare Krishna said, "But you cannot get to the top without becoming a devotee to your call area." For me, the price tag of success is devotion and diligence to your assignment in life. Apostle Paul said, *"Not that I have already attained or am already perfected; but I press on, that I may lay hold of that for which Christ Jesus has also laid hold of me"* (Philippians 3:12). Dedication requires you to press on even if you don't feel like it.

The speed of your breakthrough can be limited or accelerated by your dedication and the price you are willing to pay for it. The greatest weapon of the devil against you is indolence, but devotion is your greatest weapon over him. Dedication is the power to see every dream come true. The key code is not only in the opportunity but hard work and commitment. Getting to the top requires perseverance and sacrifice from when you're in isolation. The hard work is done when you are in the limelight; it is always dark before the light. In life, there are no bypasses or shortcuts to the top. It will take devotion, dedication, and hard work to get to the top.

Order is Established

To be established means to have been in existence for a long time and therefore recognised and generally accepted. In isolation, God calls you to order. One of the significant ways to get to the top is by establishing yourself. Most leading figures in the body of Christ have not been established long enough to command authority. We have hurried frontline leaders who think this is a fashion parade. They come up with words like "branding", "social media presence" "trends" and the like. All of these cannot make you successful or accomplished. Having a virtual following of one hundred thousand people does not connote establishment.

I once drove through Liverpool, and seeing a 200-year-old factory humbled me. To me, it is an epitome of establishment. Many churches have mega buildings but shallow leaders. You build to survive the winds of change and modernisation. Can your child still listen to your tape or speech ten years from now? Can your ministry endure if the clouds unfold their wings of strife? Can your marriage or family last after a heavy downpour of tribulations? In your night seasons, build structures, not hype. In your training day, craft longevity for yourself, not propaganda. I have seen young men and women who have been eyeing their leaders' pulpit but when they got there, they were echoes, not voices. Be established if you want to avoid this. Study to show yourself approved and establish yourself as a child of God.

The greatest of us is not the one with a beautiful logo or a nice clothing line. The greatest of us are those who are established for tomorrow. Life is more than fashion, and the ministry is more than titles. The race is a long-distance run, not a sprint. Therefore, my good friend, build your endurance, not fans. Build up fortitude, not followers. There is a correlation between an established person and a person of purpose. The majority of successful people are primarily focused on a particular field of interest. Establishment makes you an institution. In life, the best form of correction is direction. If you want to correct something or somebody, direct them. And when you are established, you become an immovable source of strength to others.

Order is Regulated

To regulate means to control or maintain the rate or speed (of a machine or process) to operate properly. The word "regulated" also connotes controlled, adjusted, managed, balanced, set, synchronised, modulated, tuned and polished. Some people cannot move to the top, not because of a demon or an ancestral curse but because they are not regulated. Some characteristics of metal which describe who regulated people are. They are either malleable or ductile.

The Merriam-Webster Dictionary defines malleable as:

1. Capable of being extended or shaped by

beating with a hammer or by the pressure of rollers.
2. Capable of being altered or controlled by outside forces or influences.
3. Having a capacity for adaptive change.

Some of those on the corridors of power find it hard to adapt and abound because they are not malleable. They cannot be tuned, managed or beaten into shape. Most people with specific backgrounds can't adapt to change because they are not flexible. Most people in privileged positions are either hammered or pressured into these places. Sadly, our churches and power centres have been signed "out of order".

The Merriam-Webster Dictionary also defines ductile as:
1. Capable of being drawn out into wire or thread.
2. Easily led or influenced.
3. Capable of being fashioned into a new form.

Getting to the top will require you to be regulated. And to be regulated means the following:

To be able to be extended.
- Beaten into shape with the 'hammer of life.'
- You can be altered or controlled as a person.
- Have the capacity to adapt to change.
- Can be drawn into threads (strands, sequence, lace, and categorisation).
- Can be led or can follow simple instruction.
- Will have the influence (impact, effect, or impression) of their leader.
- They are cables that have been transformed, framed or fabricated into new forms.

The Non-Negotiables of Order

1. Have Clarity

To reach the top, you must have clarity about your intentions and actions. No great person arrives on the shores of greatness easily. You must be clear about the fact that sometimes the waiting can last a lifetime. By the time it shows up, your energy might have been spent. I once saw a woman in her mid-seventies at her newly opened restaurant. She was bouncing like a teenager, and she said to me, "I have been waiting a long time for this." And she added that it was worth the wait.

You can easily step out of order when you lack clarity. The moment Gehazi lost clarification, he lost the most incredible opportunity a servant could have. Elisha, Joshua and the apostles had clarity. The moment Peter fumbled, he was put in order. The moment your vision becomes blurry, you are in for a long drive. Clarity is the signpost on the wall.

2. Stay Focused

In the place of isolation, God will have to wire into you order, organisation and composition. You will be required to be on the alert and be vigilant. These are the non-negotiables of divine order. When you start thinking you are better than your leader or you will do a better job than your manager, you lose focus. Anytime you think you are better than your parents, your pastor or your immediate line manager, that is a disorder in motion. No matter how eloquent, educated or erudite you think you are, you cannot be above the people that brought you in. When you come in as a greenhorn, the people you meet first will always be better and sometimes more equipped than you are. Stay focused; don't allow modernisation and technology fool you. Don't take an accent for intelligence. Your parents have an accent that does not beat down their worth, wisdom, experience and intelligence. The same applies to your manager or pastor.

Stay focused on the job at hand. If you don't define your core beliefs, you will lose focus. We had a lovely gentleman working within our church many years ago. He had a pastoral call on his life. I liked him, and he had served in our church for a long time. We had lots of time together, student-teacher relationship. My prayer was to hand over the church to him. In one year, I saw a shift in his focus and attitude. Although he was in church and we did the usual stuff together, I felt a significant shift in his focus. Sometimes, your leader can see what you cannot see. Just as Judas was an apostle, John the beloved was also an apostle.

Take a look at 2 Kings 5:25-27 (MSG) — *He returned and stood before his master. Elisha said, "So what have you been up to, Gehazi?" "Nothing much," he said. Elisha said, "Didn't you know I was with you in spirit when that man stepped down from his chariot to greet you? Tell me, is this a time to look after yourself, lining your pockets with gifts? Naaman's skin disease will now infect you and your family, with no relief in sight."* Gehazi walked away, his skin flaky and white like snow.

Elisha's question could be rephrased as "Weren't my spirit with you when you took those gifts?" Elisha knew Gehazi had lost focus a long time ago. In isolation, you might be tempted to lose sight of the main thing, but you must be careful. Maintaining focus is crucial to your assignment in life. What you set your eyes on, you will eventually become. The day you start having a double mind, you are in serious trouble.

3. Stay Confident

There are moments in life when you may lose your belief due to delayed blessings. I was once like that. I didn't want to preach or go to church because I had lost confidence in many things. When you are shut in God's incubator and you are going through some moments, you might sometimes lose your conviction and competitive edge. To stay in charge, you must be confident. The day you lose confidence, you will be out of order. This is nonnegotiable if you want to attain greatness. There is a difference between confidence and complacency. Do not allow what you are not capable of to interfere with what you are good at.

Confidence is not a gain in one year; it is a dose of victories over your daily battles. Every success is a building block of confidence. When you are confident, it means you are calm, unruffled, equanimous and level-headed. This will help you to discharge your duties with passion and enthusiasm. Sadly, many have missed some opportunities because of lack of passion and confidence.

You can tell if somebody will get to the top when you see their conviction about service, divine order and timing. At times, your wife, colleagues or even close associates will advise you to move out of order. They will tell you to do something for yourself. They will be your Ahithophel; their advice in your valley of decisions will sound good on the surface, but they are not. Be confident in your convictions about your assignment, and humbly ask God for a staying power.

4. Stay Disciplined

Some people have missed their timing, opportunity, and moments in life because of a lack of discipline. The derivative of discipline is a major determining factor in getting to the top. There has been more leadership, marriage, and life wreck caused by lack of discipline. The power of a disciplined life will thrive on any grounds in life. Discipline is doing what you know must be done, although it doesn't feel like it. Vision gets you started, but discipline keeps the vehicle of your life going. Discipline can turn mediocrity into a great accomplishment. It is the magnetic force that makes men and women virtually impossible to stop. Whenever you see a man of discipline, it is a derivative that reverts talents and abilities into outstanding accomplishments. Discipline is the primary key to getting to the top. The gap between dreams and fulfillment is discipline. The difference between achievement and hustling is not a degree but discipline.

Ability without discipline is a tragedy waiting to happen. With lots of power, more money, and bundles of opportunities without the element of discipline, a wreck is about to happen. Getting to the top is nothing more than a few simple disciplines observed every day. Our generation likes the idea of success and stardom, but self-discipline is creating the situation. Discipline and self-restraint are the principal qualities of creating the tomorrow you want today. There is no ideal formula for greatness in life other than discipline.

Discipline is the refinery by which any endowment you are given becomes a success and a blessing to your generation. The power to flatten a mountain, the ability to cross a river, and the moment to overcome a life crisis are not in more money or more power but the discipline. Discipline is the utmost characteristic of any man or woman you have seen made it in life.

5. Stay Humble

In the place of isolation, God gives you the spirit of humility. Christ learnt obedience and humility through his experiences (Hebrew 5:8). Similarly, we go through some phases in life that make us humble. Arrogance makes you synthetic, but humility makes you authentic. Humility is the truth, but pride is a trap. Pride always goes before a fall. A humble person is often dependable and trustworthy. The biblical story I love most is Abraham's humility when the angels visited him. He had many servants yet he made haste to prepare their lunch and stood by as a waiter. It doesn't take a lot to be humble, but it costs much to be arrogant. Sometimes I see talented people with narcissistic and egoistic traits. Let your most excellent portrait be like Moses. He was described as the meekest man on earth. *Now the man Moses was very humble (gentle, kind, devoid of self-righteousness), more than any man who was on the face of the earth* (Numbers 12:3 AMP).

Moses was commissioned to rescue the Israelites from the grip of slavery. He split the red sea with his rod. He oversaw the tragic end of Pharaoh and his chariots in the red sea. He placed a demand on heaven's bakery house and fed the people with manna. He saw God and spoke to Him. He was the only man who used a tablet with God's writing. He was successful in ministry, business and military power. He walked in power and glory. Yet he was described as a man who *"was very humble (gentle, kind, devoid of self-righteousness) more than any man on the face of the earth"*. This is what God does when he puts us in isolation. He breaks us so much that we would be devoid of pride and arrogance. Moses was the most humble man on earth in the world he lived in. Stay humble.

6. Stay Spiritual

Don't allow anything to usurp your spiritual senses. When people are kept in confinement, they often lose their ability to reason spiritually.

Discernment is our power detector when it comes to truth and error. It helps us to make precise distinctions in thinking about truth and falsehood. It arms you to take a biblical stand against the barrage of falsehoods. It is sad that many Christians are unable to measure what they are taught against the standard of God's word. Sharpen your spiritual sense so that you can make informed decisions in life. Discernment is a supernatural tool God gives us as we walk through life. The Merriam-Webster dictionary defines discernment as "The quality of grasping and comprehending what is obscure; skill in discerning; an act of perceiving or discerning something." Many people have missed it in life because of a lack of discernment. Never allow your pain to obscure your ability to decipher spiritual dynamics. Discernment is your protection against deception. It helps you to distinguish between what is probable and what is improbable. People can be honestly wrong about a decision and not know they are missing the mark. Discernment is like the high beam that casts enough light for you to see potholes that your standard lights would have missed at night.

> *"Therefore, give to your servant an understanding heart to judge Your people, that I may discern between good and evil. For who is able to judge these great people of yours?"* **1 Kings 3:9**

You need these two things: an understanding heart and discernment between good and evil if you want to succeed. Charles Spurgeon said, "Discernment is not simply telling the difference between right and wrong; rather, it tells the difference between right and almost right." Discernment is God's signal of intervention, and it's never about fault-finding. Those who are emotionally impoverished are devoid of discern-ment in choosing people and maximising their opportunities.

7. Stay Responsible

Responsibility is the act of responding to divine ability. In the Bible, elevation was relatively proportional to service and responsibility. No man or woman ever served truly without receiving assistance. With the merit you give, you receive merit too. Your responsibility often measures your promotion. How high you go depends on your ability to handle more. Many of us are not responsible with the little given to us, yet we want the big things of life. Many people will justify why things didn't work out other than accept that they are irresponsible. Your responsibility correlates with your ability. The game's rule is that you will never be promoted from a place until you are responsible for where you are.

One of my friends in Ghana was pastoring a not-so-big church, but he has proven to be responsible over the years. And God opened a new chapter of a great church for him. Sometimes, you will be required to be accountable, and that will be your platform for promotion. If you have not proven yourself for the next level, don't crave bigger and better things. Stay responsible in what you are doing, and great doors will be open to you.

8. Be Available

One of the things that amazes me is how our world has changed from the world I grew up in — technology, influx of information and social media. We had no time to waste in those days because there weren't many activities taking our attention. But today, it has become a struggle to be available to our families, jobs and even to the call of God. You might have heard that it is not your ability but your availability. There are many gaps at the top because only a few people are available. I always find it difficult to understand why people lose interest and walk away from a job, a church and even a mentor. There are many 'breakaway churches', 'walk away members, 'the stay-at-home parishioners and the 'not concerned leaders' who are still vying to get the top. But God does not use people who are hypersensitive and cannot deal with their immaturity, so they blame everybody but themselves.

Passion is the evidence of your availability. Many people don't want to be there, but they want the accolades that come with it. If you are overlooked, you don't walk away. In life, it is not your talent but your availability that matters. When you are committed, God increases your capability. I have heard people say, "I am leaving this church because nobody called me"; 'I don't feel loved enough in this place." Such people are not ready for the top. The top is a lonely place to be, and God is teaching you to stay available no matter what. It does not take much power to move an obstacle but somebody who is willing and available. Be available regardless of how long it takes. Two people can see the same outcome differently. One sees it as a golden opportunity, and the other sees it as a problem. In life, success never comes as easy as we think; you must be willing to stay focused and available to a cause.

The Price of Disorder

The price we pay for disorder equals the cost of losing a war. In the military, preparation is equivalent to action. People have lost opportunities and resources because they were disorganised. Those who are organised are often viewed as nerds, so people try to avoid that label. In your quest to get to the top, order is non-negotiable. We often like to blame everybody for our unstructured lives except ourselves. Being organised is a lifetime trip, not a destination. The most reputable people are not those with lots of money or the gifted people you admire; rather, they are those who will turn up early for an appointment equipped and organised.

Organise Yourself: Joseph

There is an exciting story in the Bible about how Joseph interpreted a dream in prison for the king's baker and butler and hoped they would remember him when released. They were both released from jail and their dreams, as interpreted by Joseph, came to pass. The baker died by hanging three days after his release, but the butler was restored to active duty. Joseph tarried in prison for another two years until Pharaoh had a disturbing dream, and the butler remembered Joseph. Until that time, they were in a place of isolation, and they were all hidden from stardom. They might have aspired to get to the top of life's ladder, prove their innocence, and showcase their gifts. Their permutation with Joseph in prison remained to be seen, but this was certain about Joseph. He was an organised man.

> *Then Pharaoh sent and called Joseph, and they brought him quickly out of the dungeon; he shaved, changed his clothing, and came to Pharaoh.* **Genesis 41:14**

Many people have shown up unshaved and unkempt to the kings' table. But Joseph did three things: 1. He shaved 2. He changed his clothing, and 3. He showed up for the 'party'. This showed that Joseph was organised while in prison. An organised person is a recognised person. I have met people who complained about lack of opportunities but when an opportunity came, they did not see it because they were disorganised. Organisation is intentional. It doesn't just happen. You must premeditate on the what-ifs of life. What will you do if you are called to the statehouse for your long awaited dream? What will you do if your peers select you to give a speech on behalf of the group? When the call came, Joseph tidied up. He had lived in Egypt, and he knew the customs. He knew what the Egyptians liked, disliked, and what they considered an abomination. He knew that he must look like the part to be there. He knew he had to look like the Egyptians to rule over them. When the call came, he knew that it was a deliverance call straight away. Are you ready for your call of redemption?

Organise Your Time

In the place of isolation, time is of a great essence. Time spent cannot be regained. In isolation, you might feel the weight of the world. Over the years, I have organised my life into three simple sequences: God, family and everything else. As soon as our established order is altered, we struggle in the place of greatness. Some people are doing a lot, and they attribute it to being busy. We must understand that there are formative years and stages in everybody's life. Learn time management; it will help you in the long run. The Psalmist said, *"So, teach us to number our days, That we may gain a heart of wisdom"* (Psalm 90:12).

The psalmist prayed that he would be taught to number his days. The Hebrew word for number in the KJV is the word yada, which means to observe, care, recognise, acknowledge and be acquainted with time. Set your priorities right, and things will fall in place. Joseph, though imprisoned, must have an idea of how the whole thing would play out. He conquered time. You must as well be observant to changing times and seasons. Learn to recognise when the tide changes.

Organise Your Moment

David and his men were on their way to seek revenge for Nabal's foolish reply to David's men when they needed help. One of Nabal's servants updated Abigail about her husband's lack of spiritual sensitivity and what the repercussions might be upon David's arrival. And her response was prophetic compared to her husband's actions and response. Nabal could not organise himself; he violated divine protocol.

According to 1 Samuel 25:10-11, *"Then Nabal answered David's servants and said, "Who is David, and who is the son of Jesse? There are many servants nowadays who break away from his master. Shall I then take my bread and my water and my meat that I have killed for my shearers and give it to men when I do not know where they are from."*

Abigail knew who David was. Without hesitation and not informing her husband, she gathered food supplies and loaded them on donkeys. Then she headed out to meet the future king of Israel. She organised her moment and used it to her advantage. Many people have missed moments like that. They will sit by and blame Nabal but will not seize the moment. Many would rather destroy anybody they think has wronged them than organise their moment to reach the top. Learn to use every moment to your advantage. When the moment comes, don't waste it.

Some important attributes exhibited by Abigail:

1. Obedience

She fell on her face before him, bowing to the ground without a word. She honoured David by showing him obeisance. The power of pride was broken. She was the finished product. She was ready to be the wife of the future king. She let down her dignity as a woman and honoured him because she saw God in him.

2. Reverence

Falling at David's feet, she gave the most heartfelt petition so he would spare her husband. In isolation, God removes self-importance from you. The people God has worked on at the backside of the desert don't mind dancing naked; they don't mind serving tables and bowing to people they don't even know.

3. Honour

She did this from a heart that feared God and honoured Him. Honour without respect is incomplete; it is lip service. She showed David honour. Some people only honour you when they need something from you or when it is convenient. As soon as they get what they want, you will see their horrible attitude. After this episode, not much was said about Abigail except that she became David's wife. David married her because he saw the destiny link in her.

4. Forgiveness
Abigail did not do this as an act of revenge or vendetta against her husband. You can see this was no act of score-settling. This is a woman married to a 'fool', but she didn't allow his attitude to affect her purpose.

5. Leadership
She knew that her husband was a fool and had some shortcomings, yet she did everything to save her husband and his reputation. Many protegees think leadership means they have to be brute and rude. But leadership is management; it is governance. This woman's attitude is the epitome of what our 21st-century spouses lack. The Abigails are irreplaceable and can step up when called to do damage control.

6. Godliness
Abigail prompted the future king that his life was

in the hands of God. She told David to overcome evil with good because God would avenge him. People like Abigail are no more in the corridors of power. They are rarely found these days. Everyone is in it for what they will get; they don't mind destroying you to build their contact or gain an advantage.

7. Trust

Abigail encouraged David to allow God to decide. She was a godly woman whose trust was in God. She wasn't the revengeful type of person. Looking at the Nabal, as his name may suggest, she must be disappointed with her life, yet she seized the moment to save, not destroy. Most people will take this moment to ruin reputations.

8. Faith in the promise

Abigail only asked that David remember her when God had fulfilled everything his promises: this is proof that she was in isolation. She knew there was a platform out there for her, but she wanted somebody like Joseph to ask the men to remember him when they were restored. In these moments, don't allow revenge, disappointments and weariness to obstruct you from seeing the bigger picture. Be vigilant because portals are open on timing.

To Organise is to Anticipate

The difference between a wish and faith is anticipation. When people anticipate something, they do not let it go. They prepare for it as they expect it. Without anticipation, there can be no faith. Without hoping that you will get what you desire, your faith has no foundation, hence it cannot work for you. The first place to build your tomorrow is to be organised. To anticipate is "to foresee and act in advance of." The word comes from the Latin word 'anticipare', which means "take care of ahead of time or literally, taking into possession beforehand."

1 Samuel 9:5-8 says, *"When they had come to the land of Zuph, Saul said to his servant who was with him, "Come, let us return, lest my father cease caring about the donkeys and become worried about us." And he said to him, "Look now, there is in this city a man of God, and he is an honourable man; all that he says surely comes to pass. So let us go there; perhaps he can show us the way that we should go." Then Saul said to his servant, "But look, if we go, what shall we bring the*

man? For the bread in our vessels is all gone, and there is no present to bring to the man of God. What do we have?" And the servant answered Saul again and said, "Look, I have here at hand one-fourth of a shekel of silver. I will give that to the man of God to tell us our way."

The servant is a destiny helper. He was picked randomly; his name was never mentioned. He had no family reference or tribal alliance, yet he anticipated an offering. The servant knew there was a prophet in town, so he took some money. He persuaded Saul, the would-be king, to meet the prophet. Anticipation is an expression of faith. Isolation puts you in a state of anticipation and when you anticipate, there is a place for you at the top.

NEGOTIATION

*In life, we don't get what we want.
We are given what we negotiate.*

I hope you will be able to look back and recount every experience that has brought you this far. Your expertise and your ups and downs are the negotiating factors that have kept you going. Negotiation is a strategic discussion that resolves an issue in a way that both parties find acceptable. To negotiate is to find a way over or through something. You are negotiating with every breath you take in life. In isolation, you grow your ability to negotiate. For you to get to the top, you must learn to negotiate. Let's look at the working definition of negotiation in the context of our study.

Negotiation is a dialogue between two or more people or parties intended to reach a beneficial outcome, according to the International Project Management Association (IPMA). To negotiate is to bargain, haggle, beat down and dispute with somebody, something or a level in life. It means talking your way into an area, bidding for something, and attempting to overcome a mistake in life. To negotiate is the ability you have gained to wrestle, fight or grapple with a dimension at a place or a level above your knowledge, capacity and strength. Everything you do today requires negotiation. We often use words like bargain, get past, go around, work out a deal, haggle and beat down for negotiation. We may not have the strength to cut a deal or negotiate with certain things in life, but the experience will be helpful. You can negotiate with your gender, qualifications, race, status or experience. These tools are limited in their capacity, but God will give you the power to negotiate and navigate in life. Never waste an experience, don't discount your disappointments, and don't disdain your failures because they are your passport to greatness.

Tools for Negotiation in Life

We need certain instruments to negotiate in life, and they include:

1. Gender

Today, people have mastered the ability to negotiate to gain an advantage in life. Why do women or young girls spend hours polishing their faces and fixing their hair, even if it will take three to four hours to get it done? It is the most powerful negotiating chip on the high table to some women. Why have men's grooming business booming and aftershaves become bestsellers? It's their negotiating prowess. There are specific jobs that when a man applies for, they know they might get as compared to a woman. Similarly, women can land a particular job purely based on their feminine powers.

2. Qualifications

What are your qualifications? Who are your classmates, and what school did you attend? Are you an Oxford grad? Or Yale product? In the United Kingdom, 7% of the ruling power in the government were educated privately. In contrast, the rest of the country was educated by the state.

Life is sometimes ranked by your school, qualifications and degrees. Qualifications have become our negotiating code in the cooperative world. Two people can have a degree in the same discipline, but the difference is that the kind of university that awarded the degree makes it weighty or frivolous.

3. Race and Nationality

Today we are told there is no racism in the working environment, but it's a lie Your race or skin colour can give you negotiating power in the boardroom. I have observed it over the years as a teacher. Although some black folks have been given opportunities, they messed it up. You can be in senior management for donkey years and see another person with a different skin colour who passed you like you were never there. Their race, nationality, or accent took them to the top. Your race can become your bargaining chip in the corridors of power.

4. Status, Standing and Reputation

Your wealth will open particular doors for you. Your status affects how you are respected. Your repute holds a significant key to life's major trophy. I was in a hotel, and a YouTuber showed up to check into the hotel. The hotel staff left everyone standing to attend to this social media celebrity. As long as we live in the 21st century, the hype on social media will drive our society to its knees. Even the church is cranking up the vibe on the status and social media hype. We are the first, and we don't care whom we are harming or destroying because we need to maintain our status. Status is a negotiating code. A school, a church or people can say to you, "Look at our numbers and followers compared to so and so." This shows that the society today is status-driven.

5. Connection, Associations and Ties

Some people will cut an arm and leg to associate with a celebrities. I once sat in a friend's car, and in less than an hour, he was able to speak to almost every preacher I grew up admiring. His connection alone opens significant doors for h. They say show me your friend, and I will show you your future. Our connection and association are also our negotiating powers. I was honoured to have met the late Archbishop Benson Idahosa. I was even given an opportunity to speak in an honourable pulpit because I told a group of pastors I saw him the last day he died. They were overwhelmed by that experience. Some connections in life could be your only key to opening some doors. Watch whom God is pairing you with. This association may be needed at the negotiating table tomorrow.

6. Family, Name and Lineage

Today, people only have to mention their names, and doors will open. I am from a specific background in Ghana called the Akans. Your name speaks a lot about your value and your prestige in life. Your name, or what people sometimes refer to in the business world as goodwill, is a powerful negotiating chip in any central league table. There's a joke that goes this: "The reason Bugatti, Lamborghini, Rolls-Royce and Aston Martin don't do TV commercials is that the people who buy these cars don't sit down watching daytime soap operas on TV. You will never see a TV advert for these cars because of their brands and names." If you have a good name, it is as equal as gold. A good name is chosen rather than great riches (Proverbs 22:1). Your name or family name can be a gateway to stardom.

7. Giftings, Callings, Talents and Ability

Our giftings are determined by the several abilities God has given us. When people can do what others cannot do, it shouldn't be seen as an advantage, but grace. In this competitive generation, everything is to whose detriment. People use their God-given gifts to negotiate in life. Having a fantastic voice to sing and the ability to draw or do something innate is God's gift to you. Yet on the negotiating table, people will use that card as though it is our fault we can't sing or draw like them. This should be accredited to grace, but people use their grace to disgrace others.

8. Age, Experience or Time of Life

You will be given specific opportunities because of your time, level rank or age. These factors can aid negotiation. So, there are moments that you have to negotiate with those tons of experience you gained in your isolation. There's a place in life you can only get there if you are old enough, experienced enough and prepared enough. Negotiate with your experience, and don't make the same mistake twice.

9. Sheer will and determination

This is a negotiable tool for anyone willing to go beyond their comfort zone. If you have ever dreamt of being at the top, you must have an extraordinary amount of determination. In life, we negotiate with our ability to hold on and stick to what others give up so easily. We negotiate with our bounce-backability (the word bouncebackability was adopted into the oxford dictionary because a football in England manager once said, 'as a team, we must have a bounced back ability after we fail').

10. Elastic Faith

Some people have what they have today because of their faith in God. In isolation, what God develops in you is elastic faith. He stretches you to believe in the impossible. Elastic faith is the power of faith beyond humans. It's the faith that can be tested. It wants to do the impossible. It is the faith that moves mountains and defeats opposition. It made Zacchaeus run and sit on the Sycamore tree when others with worse conditions were still following Jesus. It makes the future present, but it is developed in isolation.

The Power of Negotiation

1. Negotiation will open dimensions beyond your level, ability, and strength
2. It can give you the best of life without struggle.
3. It is a pathway to any greatness or height in life.
4. In negotiation, you learn to bargain and can buy something beyond your means.
5. It bequeaths on your power and strength on the table of discussion*
6. There is something you can offer which is why you find yourself in that position and therefore negotiate.
7. In negotiation, you are wrangling or battling with greatness and great minds.
8. Within everybody is an innate tool given by God to negotiate: use it! You got it!
9. If you know how to negotiate in life, you become indispensable in any level of life setting.
10. Knowing how to negotiate well will save your life and the lives of others.

Our Supernatural Tool Sets for Negotiation

At any level of negotiation, there are tool sets we use to negotiate. Some men and women were plunged into isolation, and God stepped in to become their negotiator. This book is an opportunity to understand that apart from the natural ability we negotiate with, there are times it takes the supernatural and God to negotiate on our behalf.

1. God is Our Negotiator

He negotiated for David in 1 Samuel 16:6-7, which says "So it was, when they came, that he looked at Eliab and said, "Surely the Lord's anointed is before Him!" But the Lord said to Samuel, "Do not look at his appearance or his physical stature because I have refused him. For the Lord does not see as man sees; for man looks at the outward appearance, but the Lord looks at the heart."

Many people's blessings have been given to others because of supernatural misjudgement. Things to note about David's situation:

- His father did not invite him to the sacrifice when the prophet came to their house.
- His brothers didn't think he mattered in this

discussion of selecting the next king.
- Potentially, he was the "black sheep" of the family and was kept at the backside of the wilderness to look after the sheep.
- He may have heard about the coming of Samuel but didn't think it mattered.

David was in isolation, yet his name was mentioned in a gathering of men who said he was not qualified. But God was the negotiator in this discussion. God is your negotiator if you are not invited to the table. A supernatural negotiating tool kicks in when men discount you. There are a lot of young prospects whose moments have been given to someone else because a man of God got it wrong. Yet if God puts you in isolation, he has to make a day for you to be glorified, so He will step in to be your negotiator.

He negotiated for Jacob. Laban had defrauded him for twenty years. Every deal with his uncle was a deal for him to lose. He came to the table with a new contract, but it was God the negotiator this time. Laban said in Genesis 30:28, "Name me your wages, and I will give it."

God gave Jacob a plan. Like many people, Jacob would have broken ranks and left the church or the job because what was done to him was unfair. But Laban said to Jacob, 'Name me your wages, and I will give it.' You may not have been treated fairly, but be careful you don't break ranks. God respects ranks, not power. Serve generously, do your due diligence, and do your best in your assignment.

See what happened in Genesis 31:7-12

> *Yet your father has deceived me and changed my wages ten times, but God did not allow him to hurt me. If he said thus: 'The speckled shall be your wages,' then all the flocks bore speckled. And if he said thus: 'The streaked shall be your wages,' then all the flocks bore streaked. So God has taken away the livestock of your father and given them to me. And it happened at the time when the flock conceived that I looked up and saw in a dream that the rams which mated [with the female goats] were streaked, speckled, and spotted. And the Angel of God said to me in the*

> *dream, 'Jacob.' And I said, 'Here I am.'*
> *He said, 'Look up and see, all the rams*
> *which are mating [with the flock] are*
> *streaked, speckled, and spotted; for I have*
> *seen all that Laban has been doing to you.*

God gave Jacob a negotiation tool to outsmart the con. He got an idea which he used to beat Laban. God paid Jacob in isolation by giving him a fantastic dream of how to move to the top. This is what this book is about. Keep serving whoever is taking advantage of you, and pray for those who spitefully use and persecute you (Matthew 5:44). This is the hard part of the isolation experience, but you learn to make God your negotiator when you hang in there. Eventually, with fourteen significant blessings in his life, Jacob emerged as a winner. He produced the twelve tribes of Israel and outlived his oppressor and bully. Laban, the oppressor, was never heard of ever.

God negotiated for Joseph. He was thrown into a political jailhouse. Sometimes your experience explains where you are going. In this narrative, God was the principal negotiator. Joseph asked to be remembered by the recipients of his gift, but they didn't. He did his job, exercised his skills, and served. But God made Pharaoh's dream that bothered him. Some significant forces are at play on the negotiating table, and you are at the helm of the agenda. Your term of service is coming to an end, and God will step in and turn the tables in your favour. You don't need to vacate your post of service. Nobody will applaud you if you are in the middle of nowhere. Be consistent because God will turn the table around for your good. Joseph's time was up to move to the top. He needed a negotiator, and God used a supernatural (dream) toolset to unlock the moment.

> *Now it came to pass in the morning that his spirit was troubled, and he sent and called for all the magicians of Egypt and all its wise men. And Pharaoh told them his dreams, but there was no one who could interpret them for Pharaoh.*
> **Genesis 41:8**

At the point of breakthrough, some people jump ship when it looks like there is troubled water on the way. Greatness requires you to have the momentum to keep going when the going gets tough. These men above had God as their negotiator. You master how to use the negotiating tools when you are in isolation. These negotiable powers are the primary reasons we submit to mentors. There is power in waiting; it enables God to pass you the mantle.

2. Favour is Our Negotiator

Favour is our negotiator in life. It terminates suffering. It is a supernatural principle that gives you things you don't qualify for. It serves as a divine shortcut to greatness. It breaks down every limitation and boundary. What gets you to the King's table is favour. How favour negotiates on our behalf:

1. Favour changes rules, regulations, and even laws if necessary (if required) to our advantage (Esther 2:15).
2. It encompasses us as a divine protection (Psalm 5:12).
3. It will win battles and go to war on your behalf. (Psalm 44:1-3, Exodus 14).
4. Favour open the heavens over your life. Others struggle with it, but you don't (Esther 7:3).
5. Favour makes you fulfil the number of your

days (Exodus 23:25-26).
6. It will make men give you before they realise they have given you.
7. It can take you from obscurity to the limelight of God's glory (Esther 2:17).
8. Favour stirs supernatural increases and promotion in any sphere of life (Acts 2:47).
9. Favour activates restoration and restitution (Exodus 3:21).
10. Favour will connect you with people who matter in life (Esther 5:8).

3. The Presence of God is Our Negotiator

Some people enjoy the presence of God. They may not be well educated or erudite in their disposition, but there is something special about them. When Moses led Israel to the Promised Land, he demanded God's presence so they could be seen as separated people.

Then he said to Him, "If Your Presence does not go with us, do not bring us up from here. For how then will it be known that Your people and I have found grace in Your sight, except You go with us? So, we shall be separate, Your people and I, from all the people who are upon the face of the earth. (Exodus 33:15-16 NKJV)

God's presence takes up residence in every child of God who spends quality time with Him. Although we can't predict when God will make His Presence known to us, it makes us different. When you spend time resting in God's presence, you feel satisfied.

How the presence of God becomes our negotiator

1. You build your confidence and faith (Acts 4:13).
2. You are distinguished and recognised (Exodus 33:15-16).
3. There is wisdom (Proverbs 2:1-6).
4. There's peace and absolute calmness (Isaiah 26:3).
5. You have joy amid chaos (Psalm 16:11).
6. The deeds of the flesh are mortified.
7. You consistently mount up with wings and soar high on wings like the eagle whenever you are in His presence. You run and not grow weary. You will walk and do not faint (Isaiah 40:31).
8. You are at rest when the world is falling apart around you (Psalm 37:7).

4. Your Vision is a Negotiator

A man without a vision is a man without a mission. Everything we use today such as clothing, furniture, television, and handsets are products of someone's vision. If your vision comes from God, it has a mandatory provision from heaven. Do everything you can to hold on to your vision. If you invest in it, it will take you to your destination. Spend time talking about it. Find more about that dream in your heart. Every successful vision was studiously pursued. God's vision over your life is your negotiating key to the future. To unlock it, you must first spend time in God's presence to listen for His directions.

The Power of Your Vision

1. Your vision will unlock the future (Habakkuk 2:1-4).
2. Write your vision; it is your key code to the future (Acts 26:19).
3. Your vision holds the ignition to every momentum of your life.
4. Your vision is your motivator and negotiator to move forward whenever you are discouraged, distracted or disappointed by life (John 6:67-

69).
5. The vision is the antidote to the trials, rejection and persecution you are faced with in life.
6. The vision of God over your life is time constraints. It will manifest in God's time (Ecclesiastes 3:11).
7. Every vision from God is driven by faith (Habakkuk 2:4).

5. Your Inner Circle are Your Negotiators

Jesus had twelve disciples but chose three men who were His secret circle. You are as powerful as your inner circle. Your strength and progress are dependent on how valuable your inner circle is. Your inner circle can get you promoted or demoted. As you progress in life, you create an inner circle. Sometimes it is deliberate; other times, it is a divine link-up. And in most cases, where you are going determines the kind of people you attract. In isolation, we build twelve primary cycles before our opportunity knocks. These cycles are incubators; they are the paediatrician of your gifts and calling. When you break ranks, there are repercussions. The half-baked people we have today are like that because they broke away from their divine inner cycle.

What happens when you break inner circle rank?

- You incur the wrath of God. It is like stopping a cycle of supernatural production.
- You violate spiritual protocol, which has consequences for your life.
- You make yourself vulnerable and exposed, either you went too early or late.
- It's a sign of betrayal and disloyalty. The day Judas broke rank, he sold the Messiah.
- Breaking inner circle rank signifies an unresolved conflict and internal conflict.
- It connotes pride and arrogance.
- You think there's a greener pasture somewhere else. You also feel your mentors are not good enough.
- You disconnect from a holy alliance.
- You are saying their assignment in your life is done. God decides when you are ready, not you or your friends.
- You dry up, hang yourself or even get "turned" by life's events.

6. The Church is Our Negotiator

The primary thread in this book is our faith in Christ. Where would most of us be if not for the church? God picked me up in the most austere part of Ghana. My mum sold kenkey by the roadside and lived in one of the most impoverished parts of the country. It took the church, Global Revival Ministries to give me a voice to be who I am today. The church that groomed you and shaped your beliefs could be your stepping stone to who you are today.

7. Anointing is Our Negotiator

Everyone is a custodian of an anointing — the power of God unleashed over our lives to carry out His will. There are different measures of anointing. And none is received based on deception. You simply catch anointing. It is the application of oil, and it activates beauty, strength and power. Anointing triggers transformation and gives you the ability to do what others cannot do.

How can anointing become your negotiator?

1. It empowers you to deal with the devil and demonic powers (Acts 10:38).

2. It authorises you to break yokes, curses and bondages (Isaiah 10:27).
3. It endorses us to break poverty cycles in life.
4. It allows you to heal the sick and restore the soul (Mark 16:18).
5. It gives you the power to deal with invisible battles in life (Ephesians 6:12).
6. It approves us to proclaim new seasons and eras (Isaiah 55:18).
7. It bequeaths on us power to overcome limitations and break bondages, backgrounds and challenges.
8. It emboldens you to carry heavy loads and burdens.
9. It confers on you to handle elevation and upliftments.
10. It drives you to move to the next level in life.
11. It imparts on you to unlock territories, gifts, dimensions and levels.
12. It stirs our creativity and inspiration in life.

8. Commitment is Your Negotiator

As a child of God, commitment is your superpower. I urge you to examine your commitment because it is a critical key to greatness in life. Some people may never have the opportunities you have had in life, yet they are sitting at the high table because commitment is their negotiator. It's easy to confuse longevity with commitment. It means being faithful to whom or what faithfulness is required. Some people are only committed when it's convenient. It pays when you follow through to the end. And the price of commitment is equal to everything you've ever achieved. Your commitment is a necessary code to opening doors of opportunities.

Now that you have finished reading *Getting to the Top*, **I** would like you to evaluate the lessons you learnt from and pass them on to someone who may need them.

Thank you for taking the time to read this book.

God bless you!

Emmanuel Anning

www.ingramcontent.com/pod-product-compliance
Lightning Source LLC
Chambersburg PA
CBHW061634040426
42446CB00010B/1419